Stories of

ROARING
F A I T H

COMPILED AND EDITED BY
DONNA SKELL
LISA B. WORLEY ◆ BELINDA MCBRIDE
FRANK BALL

Stories of Roaring Faith
Copyright © 2018 by Roaring Lambs Publishing

Published by:
Roaring Lambs Publishing
17110 Dallas Parkway, Suite 260
Dallas, TX 75248
Email: **info@RoaringLambs.org**

Dedication

To God,
Thank You for the difference
You make in our lives.

To Garry Kinder,
Founder of Roaring Lambs Ministries,
Because of you, this book is possible.

To all the contributors of this book,
Thank you for sharing your personal testimonies
With the world.

To all the readers,
May your relationship
With our Lord Jesus Christ grow.

Introduction

About thirty-five years ago, I had the opportunity to attend a small class that taught me how to confidently and effectively share the Gospel against the backdrop of my life experiences. **It changed my life.** I learned the importance of sharing how God had proved Himself real to me.

Come and hear, all you who fear God; let me tell you what he has done for me. — Psalm 66:16

For the last several years, Roaring Lambs has been encouraging and equipping believers to effectively compose their testimony. Whether sharing one-on-one, speaking to a group, or just putting it in writing as a legacy for future generations, it is beneficial.

We will tell the next generation the praiseworthy deeds of the Lord, his power, and the wonders he has done, so the next generation would know them, even the children yet to be born, and they in turn would tell their children. — Psalm 78:4, 6

Our testimony is our opportunity to let God use the circumstances He has allowed in our life for His glory. When you can take a difficult time, show how God used it for His good and yours, then you can give Him glory for that very hardship.

When he heard this, Jesus said, "This sickness will not end in death. No, it is for God's glory so that God's Son may be glorified through it." — John 11:4

Putting your faith story together will prepare you for many opportunities to share your faith. Each day, you are more likely to realize just how many there are.

But in your hearts revere Christ as Lord. Always be prepared to give an answer to everyone who asks you to give the reason for the hope that you have. But do this with gentleness and respect. — 1 Peter 3:15

The world needs to see how real Jesus is. Times are short. Your story matters. It is the living water that others need.

Then he said to his disciples, "The harvest is plentiful but the workers are few." — Matthew 9:37

Are you ready to be used by God and be richly blessed? Tell your story of what He has done for you.

Then I heard the voice of the Lord saying, "Whom shall I send and who will go for us?" And I said, "Here am I. Send me." — Isaiah 6:8

Donna Skell, Executive Director
Roaring Lambs Ministries

Acknowledgements

My sincere thanks are extended to Frank Ball for his gracious help turning this manuscript into a book. You are a kind, generous, God-loving man, and very appreciated by this ministry.

To Dan Thompson, our graphic designer from T-Bone Designs, many thanks for all your work with Roaring Lambs, to give us such a great look. You are talented and have established our visual image. Thanks especially for a great cover for this book.

Thank you, Sherry Ryan, for your work editing the testimonies. I know you were blessed by reading them, but we are blessed by all your spelling, punctuation, and grammar corrections.

To my co-compilers and editors, Belinda McBride and Lisa Burkhardt Worley, without the two of you, this book would have never been completed. Thank you for your endless hours of reading and re-reading the stories. Thank you for your attention to the small details.

Thank you, again, to all who contributed their personal testimonies. This book is not about you, but is all about our great and awesome God we serve.

Story Power

Always be prepared to give an answer to everyone who asks you to give the reason for the hope that you have. — *1 Peter 3:15*

The Good News is what Jesus made possible when people follow Him. Christians may be hard pressed on all sides but not crushed. As the apostle Paul says in 2 Corinthians 4:8–9, we may be perplexed, but we don't need to despair. Although persecuted, we aren't abandoned. Struck down, we aren't devastated. We have peace that defies understanding (Philippians 4:7).

How will you share this Good News with those who don't know Jesus? You can't quote Scripture when people don't believe the Bible. Telling them their perception of Jesus is wrong won't change their minds. If they won't accept your truth, what can you say that might make a difference?

They will listen to your story—how you survived traumatic times. Undeniable proof of God's love and mercy is revealed through the struggle that changed you from the person you once were to who you've become. Your story is the Good News that has transforming power for others.

The power of story is the experience readers have when they feel the pain of those who have lived without hope until they found the Lord and chose to follow him.

As people read *Stories of Roaring Faith, Volume 3*, they will see how God makes a practice of mending hopelessly shattered lives. The messages are life-changing, because they show that what God has done for others He can also do for them.

Frank Ball, Assistant Director of Roaring Writers
Roaring Lambs Ministries

Table of Contents

Triggered Happy
by Linda Churchwell

The gun barrel that was rammed against my temple felt hard, hot, painful, and terrifying—yet surreal. My heart pounded my chest wall so much that I ached both physically and emotionally. My mind tried to keep up with the breakneck speed of my racing heart, but shock blocked its feeble attempt.

I could never have imagined what would happen next. Unable to give my assailants all they demanded, I heard the horrific, ominous, and mechanical "click." With the barrel at the side of my head, the cocking of his gun roared inside my ear as my perpetrator prepared to shoot. I was going to die.

The emotions I imagined I'd have when facing death were nothing like what I actually experienced. The overwhelming sensation of acceptance was unimaginable to me and impossible to explain. I had never felt this kind of acceptance before. It was an entirely new feeling. The terror that had consumed me faded, surprisingly swallowed up by a strange new sensation—peace. But why? Where had that feeling come from?

As I was growing up, my life appeared normal, from an external perspective. We were a typical middle-class family living in the United States—two parents and two kids—my older brother and me, the younger daughter. We had two cars, and we were one of the first families on the block to have a color TV. Some of our neighbors occasionally dropped by to join us as we watched a popular show, *Flipper*. I remember being dazzled by the brilliant blue water on the small square screen. Our family had good behavior during those occasions.

However, when company left, a knife was needed to slice the tension and fear. Unspoken traumas were swept underneath proverbial rugs. The "shush" stuff, never talked about, never divulged, took on its own serpent-like slithering life, and tolls were taken.

Aubrey Sr, my biological father, whom I now compassionately understand had been spawned from his own horrors of dysfunctional, violently abusive, and unhealthy parents, was an apple not far from its tree, less the violence. I lived terrified of this

1

man and could not sit in a room alone with him. If other human buffers were present, it was doable, but only then. My father managed his own inherited dysfunction by mastering the art of domination, control, and harshness. He was scary. With me being the youngest and a petite girl to boot, he felt larger than life—a huge monster to be avoided at all costs.

Consequently, on many nights I trembled uncontrollably in my bed as I listened to Dad verbally abuse the only safe, sweet spot in my life, my precious mother. Because of the tumultuous nights, I developed deep-seated anxiety disorders. I became so shy (another term for fear) that while in kindergarten I could rarely muster enough courage to ask permission to go to the bathroom. One traumatic humiliating time, I arrived home after school with poop in my red ruffled panties.

While my mother was my true love, she was afraid of her husband as well and did not stand up for me when I needed her. My older brother, who was abused by our father in other ways, slowly evolved into our dad's carbon copy. Now I had two monsters to deal with, my father and my brother, and the latter sexually abused me.

During the early seventies and at the height of the drug craze, I couldn't wait to jump into my great escape, feet first. Very little persuasion was needed to enter the world of drugs. I desperately wanted any means possible out of my pain. In the seventh grade, I was introduced to marijuana, then hallucinogenics in the eighth, amphetamines in the ninth, and inhalants and alcohol in the tenth—all in my aching attempt to find love at any cost. Sexual promiscuity also entered my life.

At times, my mom talked about God and how she believed in the Lord Jesus, but my father wanted no part of it. On occasion, when the "boss" allowed, we attended a denominational church, which was unequivocally the most boring experience of my life. I was convinced that those attending were simply waiting to be embalmed. Later, I believed the only thing I would be allowed to do if I were a Christian was eat. But then I'd be fat and still miserable.

As the high school years wound down and graduation took place, I also "graduated" from the marijuana kick and went straight for the hard stuff. In my blindness and wandering, I couldn't see

2

wasting any time. There were situations where someone would share about Christianity and Jesus, but I thought that was only for weak weirdos or the boring. The powers of darkness had me. I was all in. I was a lost, hopeless, terrified soul, who had no idea that all my answers awaited me in one perfect being.

As the years went by, my suffering intensified. I was frantically searching for love in all the wrong places, and every attempt at relief only left me emptier than before. I had promised myself early on, one thing I would never do, no matter what, was use or inject drugs with needles. I realized that "to shoot up" was a death sentence.

One Friday night as usual, I was looking for love in all the wrong places. Over a period of hours, my brother, who already used needles, talked me into using them as well. I desperately wanted my brother's love too. There was no protective covering over my life, and while my mother loved me, she didn't know how to handle these types of things and succumbed to denial.

The devil's mission in life is as the Bible tells us in John 10:10. "The thief comes only to steal and kill and destroy; I have come that they may have life, and have it to the full."

Satan is the master deceiver, and because we are lovingly made in God's image, as Genesis tells us, Satan's only mission is to destroy the very thing Jesus loves, because that is the only way God can be hurt. The devil has no power over the omnipotence of Almighty God, nor a born-again child of God. The only way the enemy can hurt God is by hurting His creation, which He passionately loves.

As the enemy's plot progressed, in college I began to shoot amphetamines (speed injected by needle) regularly. Soon I was dealing drugs, which opened an even more-depraved door in my life. Dealing brought lots of money with lots of danger. In a matter of months, I was submerged in deep and dangerous waters with the seediest of crowds. My world was filled with guns and infidelity— steeped in the utter depths of corruption. In the drug world, there are no friends—only the next "fix" (high) and the next profitable deal. While this world holds no true love in any measure, it is saturated with the most desperate of lost, bound-up souls who have no idea that true freedom even exists. I was a card-carrying member of this sad lot.

The Bible tells us in 2 Corinthians 4:3–4, "Even if our gospel is veiled, it is veiled to those who are perishing. The god of this age has blinded the minds of unbelievers, so that they cannot see the light of the gospel that displays the glory of Christ, who is the image of God."

One evening at home, after being awake for three days straight without sleep or food, I was feeling extremely ill from coming down off drugs. A well-known drug dealer (whom we'll call John) came by to pay money he owed me. We talked a short time, and I walked John to the door. When I opened the door to let him out, two men with guns stood in my doorway. My immediate thought was that the men were there for John, because he was a notorious dealer and I was a small player.

As I said before, there are no true friends in this world. One of the men hit John in the face with the butt of his gun, and John took off running. He simply left me standing there. I thought for sure they would run after John, but instead, they pushed their way into my apartment. They were there for me.

The two men threw me onto the sofa and told me they wanted all my money and drugs. As it turned out, I had made a deposit at my bank that day and didn't have all the cash they were expecting. I gave them all the drugs I had, but they were angry, strung out, wanting more. They shoved me into the bedroom and demanded all my jewelry, but that still wasn't enough. They were crazed and furious, which leads back to where we began. They thought I was lying to them.

What they didn't know is that in my deepest depravity, weeks earlier I'd begun calling out to the Lord Jesus Christ and was reading the red print in the Bible that my mother had loaned me. They didn't know about the weeks I had been throwing on clothes, dragging myself to my car, driving to whichever church I found, and walking into the sanctuary. I'd been sitting on the back row, wondering if there truly was a God and a Savior. Were they real?

Back to the scene of the crime. When the man cocked his gun to kill me, I didn't know the power and authority in Jesus' name. But I said to them in a very low voice, "I swear to God, I'm not lying." When I said, "God," the man dropped his gun from my head. He and the other intruder ran from the back of my apartment and out the front door, as if something or someone terrified them. That was over thirty years ago, and to this day, I'm convinced that those men saw a huge guardian angel.

I knew the Lord Jesus Christ saved my physical life that day. It was a miracle. I had not given myself to Him yet, but I had been searching for Him, and sweet friends, that is all it takes for His huge heart of love, mercy, and compassion to come for us. When I did surrender control of my life to my Lord Jesus, He filled me with His Spirit. A power—a force—charged through my entire body, and in an instant, my spiritual eyes were opened.

For about an hour, I was on a euphoric "high" in the Spirit. No drugs, no man, no personal friend—nothing had come close to the perfect peace and indescribable love in which I had been overwhelmingly enveloped. During that time, the Lord opened my eyes again and showed me that for every single gift He created for His children, Satan has a counterfeit. God offers us peace while Satan gives us temporary, artificial highs via drugs and alcohol. God gives us perfect love, and Satan offers false security, empty relationships, and conditional pseudo love, ending in betrayal and brokenness. Jesus gives us true life on Earth and eternal life in Heaven, wrapped in total perfection. Satan only brings death and eternal misery.

I awoke the next morning a free person. All the cravings and addictions had vanished. I had no desire for drugs, alcohol, or the people I had been with. While I had tried to read the Word before, I could never understand it. Now, when I opened the Bible, the words on the pages exploded in understanding, light, and revelation. When I walked outside, the colors in the sky, trees, and flowers were exponentially vivid and alive. Most importantly, I was filled with a peace I had never dreamt possible. I had fallen deeply in love with my Lord. I was on fire and could barely contain my joy. I'd finally come home. I'd come home to where I was always meant to be.

The Bible tells us, "For God so loved the world that he gave his one and only Son, that whoever believes in him shall not perish but have eternal life. For God did not send his Son into the world to condemn the world, but to save the world through him. Whoever believes in him is not condemned, but whoever does not believe stands condemned already because they have not believed in the name of God's one and only Son" (John 3:16–18). Jesus also says,

"Very truly I tell you, no one can see the kingdom of God unless they are born again" (John 3:3).

Giving your life to Christ is the smartest, most beautiful decision you will ever make. You can simply turn your heart to Jesus now, by repeating the following prayer with me:

"Dear Lord Jesus, I believe you are the Son of God, that you died on the cross for my sins, that you rose from the dead three days later, and that you are Lord. Please forgive me for all my sins, and be my Lord and Savior. Fill me with your Holy Spirit now. Take my life and make something beautiful out of it for Your glory. Thank you, Father, that I am now your child. In Jesus name I pray. Amen."

When I prayed, the Lord heard my cries for help and pulled me out of the deep waters that led to death to a new place that is free of addiction and full of the love for which I'd always searched. Through my belief in God's Son Jesus, I am now on solid ground and stand transformed forever.

Linda Churchwell is an award-winning author of the "Sir Winston's" novel series, including LOOPHOLE...Leaps & Hounds, endorsed by the Humane Society. In recognition of her overall work, Linda received a Literary Star in Hollywood's Walk of Fame in Los Angeles, California. For many years, Linda was also Founder and President of the global pet accessory design firm, "Lady Churchwell's Inc." She's a leader in her church and is legislated as an animal advocate with the Texas Human Legislation Network. Reach her at LindaChurchwell.com.

Thoughts to Ponder
from Triggered Happy

1. You will never find true love in the wrong places.

2. The love of God changes your desires.

3. Exchange your piece of the world for peace everlasting.

What do you need to be rescued from?

Be alert and of sober mind. Your enemy the devil prowls around like a roaring lion looking for someone to devour. — 1 Peter 5:8

The Cosmic Puppet Master
by Shannon Ray

I remember the beginning as vividly as most people remember their first kiss, their first love, or their first heartbreak. The place is Aschaffenburg, Germany, and the year is 1976. I'm in my bed sleeping, safe and sound, or so I thought. Blood curdling screams violently awakened me from my slumber, and at that point I realized I was the one screaming. My parents rushed to my bedside to comfort me and investigate the meaning of my screams. Mom and Dad tried to soothe my shaking body by telling me it was only a nightmare.

My parents were unable to see what I saw. In my bedroom, on the windowsill, were both an intruder and a friend. The intruder, which I later came to know as "the enemy of my soul" was no taller than a Barbie doll, clothed in all red, with a pitchfork in his right hand. He stood across from the friend I later came to know as "the lover of my soul." This friend was dressed in all white, almost glowing. His face never manifested clearly enough for me to see, but the sense of peace and love I felt emanating from Him drew me to Him in a way a five-year-old mind could never articulate.

The friend beckoned with an outstretched arm, as if He lassoed me with an invisible string and was pulling me to Him. As I was nearing to take His outstretched hand, I heard the intruder in red whisper four little words: "She will be mine." As he said the scariest words ever uttered, he moved his right hand forward to pierce the left side of the man in white with his pitchfork while repeating the ominous phrase. The friend in white was smiling and reaching out to pull me into the safety of His arms. In an instant, the intruder in red was after me, and the friend in white would give His life to save mine. It was terrifying. That is when the screaming began. "I don't want to be his. Oh, please. I don't want to be his."

I woke before the pitchfork violated flesh. Some attribute this scene to an overactive imagination of a girl who had heard one too many Bible stories, but that simply was *not* the case. You see, I wasn't raised in church. I hadn't been to any Sunday school classes. Looking back, I know this was when my "good work" began.

My dad was a sergeant and a medic in the U.S. Army, assigned to duty in Germany, where we lived in government housing. I routinely saw tanks driving outside our window. I unabashedly blurted out, "When I grow up, I am going to be a tank driver."

Immediately, as was his custom, Dad promptly brought me back to reality with one simple sentence. "Shannon, they don't let women drive tanks."

Devastated, I asked, "Why not?"

Dad responded with a smile and the facts, just like always. "Because tanks go to combat, and the Army does not allow women in combat."

Defiantly, I responded with, "Oh, yeah. Well then, I will be the first female tank driver in combat." If boys were allowed to do something, then girls should be allowed to do it too.

We moved back to the States the following year. When I was eight, our family visited Granny in Tennessee. She was a sweet, quiet, loving woman of God whose faith was deep, demonstrated through her words and deeds. During the visit, Granny took me to Vacation Bible School at a local Baptist church, where I first heard of a need for a Savior named Jesus. An altar call was given, and I accepted Jesus as my Savior. Seeds of faith were sown.

Matthew 13:5, 20–21 says, "Some fell on rocky places, where it did not have much soil. It sprang up quickly, because the soil was shallow. The seed falling on rocky ground refers to someone who hears the word and at once receives it with joy. But since they have no root, they last only a short time. When trouble or persecution comes because of the word, they quickly fall away."

I heard the Word and received it with joy, but it was never nurtured by my parents so it could grow. My time with Granny was over, so the seed dried up. I had already made big decisions in my eight-year-old life. After seeing various situations caused by my oldest brother, who broke my parents' hearts, I knew for certain that I wasn't going to have kids, nor was I going to get married. And without Jesus, I was going straight to Hell.

Sometime in my senior year of high school, I realized that college was *not* for me. Enter the dreams of five-year-old Shannon driving a tank. The time came to tell my parents that the thought of college made me want to heave, and I wanted to join the Army. They weren't shocked. I was never a typical girly girl. I preferred playing Army over playing house. I felt so ugly that I knew I'd never get married, nor did I want to, not after all I saw in high school. I believed men only wanted sex, and I was so much more than that.

Besides, married people had kids, and I disliked kids. Pregnant women made me shiver at the sight. The thought of expanding my body to carry a child was madness. If I ever did have children, I would adopt them.

With my parents' approval, I took the military entrance exam. I chose the U.S. Navy. After all, sailors had cute uniforms. Early in 1989, I signed the papers for the career I had dreamed of since age five. Military life would begin on December 27. The Navy was all I lived, breathed, and dreamed for the remainder of high school. God was but a distant memory. Just to be clear, I never denied Him, but I had no relationship with Him. His laws were *not* written on my heart. I worked at McDonald's to pay for my pickup truck, which was my pride and joy.

After graduation from high school, I just had to bide my time until December. However, life can change in the blink of an eye. I have visible scars on my body and a piece of glass in my forearm to remind me.

The only recollection I have is leaving my house, angry with my mom. It was her forty-second birthday. She wanted me to stay home that night to rest. I now believe God was warning her to discourage me from going to the gym to work out. It was part of my regular routine, so I'd be fit once I hit boot camp. I left the house angry, because I was an "adult" and was tired of being told what to do. I stormed out and took off in a huff in my Mazda pickup. Fifteen minutes later, I was fighting for my life.

Eyewitnesses say I wasn't driving recklessly, and they weren't sure why I ended up crossing the median of the divided highway, flipping my pickup end-over-end three times, finally coming to rest upside down.

Upon impact, my truck spun ferociously, and my body was catapulted approximately fifty-two feet from my truck into oncoming traffic. But God is a good and merciful protector. By God's grace, I didn't get hit by passing cars, and the first eyewitness to stop was an Emergency Room trauma nurse from Houston, Texas. She was on her way to St. Louis for a conference about trauma medicine.

10

The second person who stopped kept me from standing up, as I began to slowly bleed to death internally. She was the secretary for the superintendent of the school where I had graduated. I had been her aide my last semester, and I respected her.

The third person to stop was an off-duty Emergency Medical Technician who helped the nurse stabilize me until the ambulance arrived. On the way to the hospital, my vital signs stopped three times. Upon arrival, I was treated by a U.S. Army combat surgeon, who on his days off, moonlighted as an ER physician.

I was rushed to surgery to stop the bleeding. They feared it was my pancreas but were horrified to realize it was my liver that was destroyed. Because they couldn't get the bleeding to stop, I was care-flighted to a major trauma hospital in St. Louis. Dr. Douglas Hanto spent the next twelve hours and seventeen units of blood repairing my liver, ruptured so badly that a third was removed, giving me a 25 percent chance of survival.

The doctor told my parents I had a 50/50 chance of survival if I didn't go into liver failure in the next twelve hours. God went ahead of me and put every single one of those life-saving people in place. I am forever humbled by His mercy and love.

During their entire drive to the hospital, my parents prayed and begged God to spare my life. For years after learning that, I bitterly thought, *God saved my life but attached a life full of unrelenting chronic pain, miscellaneous medical issues that spring up even to this day, and Hepatitis C.*

The physical scars healed, and by God's grace, I have no recollection of anything that happened minutes prior to the accident or during the following week. My first recollection was waking up in a hospital bed, the whole left side of my head shaved, the rest of my hair in a braided, twisted, blood-filled knot that was eventually cut out, leaving me looking like a victim of Three Mile Island. I had a feeding tube in my nose, tubes to keep my lungs inflated, four tubes that reminded me of cows' udders hanging from my abdomen, and a catheter. Worst of all, there were sixty-four staples in the shape of a cross littering my entire stomach.

When I was able, I spoke the first thing on my mind. "Do I still get to ship out December 27? Is my truck okay?" All hope was not lost, or so I thought.

To keep my spirits up, my parents lied and said yes, I was still able to ship. Upon my insistence and the doctor's disapproval, I was released on August fourth, only to return to the hospital the next day. Fluid was filling my lungs. I had developed a staph infection, and I was again fighting for my life. God was still but a distant cousin to me.

My career was on hold before it even started. The U.S. Department of Defense deemed that the collapsed lungs were too much of a risk, and I had to wait one year to allow my lungs to strengthen. I was devastated, instantly bitter, and I self-imploded. God was no longer my friend. As a matter of fact, I hated Him. What loving Father rips away the one thing she ever wanted? After all, I was the good kid in the family. I graduated high school, didn't get pregnant, didn't drink or do drugs, and was obedient to my parents.

Why was I being punished?

What was the point of remaining a "good girl?"

I came out of my pity party long enough to pick up the pieces of my broken dream and glue it back together—to find a way out of the hell that had become my life. One thing led to another, and I started x-ray technology school in August 1990. This was one year and one month after my life-altering car wreck. But God was good all the time, and all the time God was good. He had pursued me my whole life, starting at age five. My heart desired to know Him. I even asked Him to be King, but because no one ever mentored me in the Word, I was a lost sheep. Little did I know that Jesus was coming to gather me into His flock. It took years for me to hear His voice and respond, but praise Him, He is relentless.

Remember, I imploded—evidenced by my drinking and partying with boys. I was loved and discarded one too many times, and I screamed out to this God I despised. I boldly let my demands be known to the One I knew existed, but by no means believed was all loving. "If You really love me," I said, "You'd send me a man who loved me for me. I don't care what he looks like, how much money he has, what his baggage is. He just has to love me for me." I soon learned that God listens to prayer, and I should be careful with how specific I was.

My dad got a new boss at work. The new boss was the answer to my prayer, the one to personify the love of Christ to me every day in a way that was real and tangible. Terry and I dated secretly until we were sure it would work out between us. We married in 1993.

12

Terry demonstrated time-after-time his desire to love me for me and that he was the one sent to answer my prayer. The clincher was when he told me he already had two children and couldn't father children with me. Remember, I didn't want kids. This God I hated answered my prayer, but not without a string attached. At least that's how I saw it.

I loved his sons from the moment I met them. How could I not? They were part of the man I loved, but they had a mother. Terry's ex-wife was a string that the Cosmic Puppet Master could use to wreak havoc into my fairy tale marriage at any given time.

In 1995, my parents convinced me to read a book titled *The Third Millennium.* I was miraculously and instantaneously convicted of my sin. I told Terry we were going straight to Hell and made him read the book. Once he finished, he placated my fears the only way he knew how, by agreeing with everything I said. I love this man.

I demanded he talk to that chick in his office with the funky hair and tattoos and find out what church she went to so we could check it out. I told him we were going to burn in Hell if we didn't get right with Jesus. Thus begins our journey to know Jesus. We attended a Bible church in Dallas, and within a year were baptized and committed our lives to serve a living, holy God. But I still didn't know him personally.

In 1996, when I was twenty-four, Terry's oldest son came to live with us, making me a full-time mother of a thirteen-year-old boy. Out of necessity, God unleashed a maternal instinct in me that could rival a mother bear protecting her cubs. Jay and I grew closer than ever while Terry's other son, Chris, grew apart from us. I quickly tired of sharing Jay with Terry's ex-wife. The maternal instinct was now alive and well and became a force I could no longer reckon with on my own. I announced to Terry that I wanted to have a child with him, a child I wouldn't have to share with his ex. I was jealous. I didn't see it then, but it's so clear now. God *uses all* things for good for those who love Him.

God used this unyielding obsession to prepare me for the two children He desired for us. I'd love to tell you it was quick, easy, and without incident, but I can't. I mean, after all, that's not how God works to refine us, is it?

Six medically aided attempts at conception using artificial insemination failed. Another string from the Cosmic Puppet Master dangled in front of me and quickly entangled me. It was the string of the desire to have a child with the man I loved, and the inability to get pregnant by him because of the vasectomy his ex had insisted on before she left him. This was coupled with complications from my car accident.

Again I found myself angry at God, but this time I struggled with feeling guilty. He was changing my heart toward Him. My head knowledge of God, Jesus, and the Holy Spirit was growing in truth and spirit, but my heart was still stony and icy. I desperately wanted to experience the "joy of my salvation" and the "peace that surpasses all understanding," but it was years before that happened.

God had work to do on my hard, calloused, prideful heart. Seeing a pregnant woman once made me shiver, but it now made me mourn for days over what I would never have. Anger and bitterness grew and made its way out of my mouth as spiteful, snide comments hurled viciously toward my adoring, loving, peace-making husband.

Why could I not break these strings that held me to this God who made me feel like a broken and used marionette? Screaming in contempt, I approached God's throne with my demands. In blind faith with a stony heart, I reached out to God, begging Him to quench the desire for a child. The heartbreak I was suffering was unbearable. Right there in my car, having my usual temper tantrum, He answered with a clear small voice in my fragile spirit. *Oh, you're going to be a mom. You're just not going to give birth.* What was that God? Did I hear you correctly? At that moment from my car radio, I first learned of The Bair Foundation, the organization that facilitated the delivery of God's promise to me. I promptly dismissed it as a weird coincidence, another likely disappointment, and changed the radio station.

Depression set in, and tears flowed freely. I was only physically present with my husband and son. I could think of nothing but having a baby. For the second time, I found myself in my car, railing at God about how unfair He was. Gently in my spirit I was told, *You're going to be a mom. You're just not going to give birth.* Again I heard the *same* commercial for The Bair Foundation.

This time I listened. The new Christian-based organization was seeking foster parents. Three months later, we finished our required classes to become foster parents with the state of Texas. This God

14

thing was finally working.

On March 10, 1999, just two days before our last class was completed, we received a phone call. I was expecting teenagers. I was shocked and overwhelmed to learn the placement was a baby and its sibling. That's all I needed to hear. I accepted the placement, called Terry, and was met with questions.

"How old? Boy or girl? What race?"

"I don't know," I said. "I didn't ask and didn't care. These are our kids."

On Saturday, March 13, we met our answered prayers. Seven-year-old Joseph and ten-month-old Jazmyn, who was born on the same Mother's Day when I gave up all hope of ever being a mom, the date of my last failed artificial insemination.

God had gone before us and made this the easiest process in the history of adoptions. The parental rights were terminated in May, and the adoption was finalized on December 21, 1999. God gave me a gift, free from the puppet strings this time, or so I thought.

Almost immediately after the adoption was final, the real Joseph showed up to the party, a black-tie affair. He was like an uninvited guest in bibbed overalls and manure-covered shoes. Therapist after therapist, diagnosis after diagnosis, our lives were forever being riddled with the bullets of a war that wouldn't see peace for more than a decade. Another string from the Cosmic Puppet Master imprisoned my heart. Jazmyn was the blessing, but Joseph was a different story.

The next eleven years were spent oscillating between anger, pity, bitterness, happiness, laughter, and love. Life was hard, and to make matters worse, it was lonely. No one understood the brokenness due to Joseph's previous abuse. We were given advice that harmed more than helped and condemned instead of confirmed.

Through all this, God remained faithful to refine me and do a good work in me. Terry and I struggled to make heads or tails of life, but one thing was for sure: God was teaching me about unconditional love. Terry's love for me never wavered. He was strength for me when I was ready to throw in the towel. He was compassion for me when I was empty. He was the embodiment of biblical love, while I was wrestling the demon that haunted me, whispering in my ear, *She will be mine.* The Holy Spirit fought for me when I couldn't fight for myself.

In my stony heart, I still believed God was a Cosmic Puppet Master who was toying with my strings. I was ashamed of the feelings I had toward Joseph and revealed them to very few people. Mercifully, God brought two women who were going through similar circumstances with their adoptive children. One could empathize with me, and the other had a heart to obey God. She had the ability to listen, pray, and point me back to Him every chance she got. Remarkably, this woman spoke truth to me in such a gentle, loving manner that I was eager to be in her presence. She was the *only* person who ever took an interest in my spiritual growth. She prayed for me relentlessly, and she is still very much a part of my journey.

I finally came to know my Savior, Jesus. I now understand the end of the dream I had at age five. Jesus' outstretched hand grabbed mine before the intruder-in-red pierced His side. And with the tiny seed of faith I had as a five-year-old girl, I screamed not to be taken by the enemy. This encounter fell on good soil, as mentioned in Matthew 13, and took root. God never gave up on me, and that tiny seed of faith continues to grow. I eagerly wait to see how God will continue to perfect me until the day of Christ Jesus.

I no longer view God as the Cosmic Puppet Master who pulls my strings for His twisted pleasure. Today, I see God as a loving Father who untangles the mess I've made of the strings that bind us together. God uses those wonderful, invisible strings so He and I can walk together, dancing along the way in times of happiness, and holding me up when I am so low that I can't lift my head to look up at Him and ask for help.

I love Him more than words can express.

Shannon Ray was born in a town that ceased to exist in 1994. This is just one of many things that mark Shannon's life as uniquely different, even from that of her own family. On the normal side, she recently celebrated her 25th wedding anniversary to a man God sent in answer to her prayers, even while she denied God's love for her. She and her husband, Terry, homeschooled two of four of their children and are now enjoying being empty-nesters.

Thoughts to Ponder
from The Cosmic Puppet Master

1. Difficult situations are a tool God can use to draw us closer to Him.

2. God is not a Cosmic Puppet Master who desires havoc in our lives.

3. God is a loving Father who untangles our messes.

How do you see God?

Being confident of this, that he who began a good work in you will carry it on to completion until the day of Christ Jesus. — Philippians 1:6

Hope in the Darkness
by Alynda Long

The product of an affair started in a bar, somewhere in one of the Carolinas. I have no memories of my father as a little girl, because my mother fled to her parents to escape physical, emotional, spiritual, and sexual abuse at his hands. Although I longed for a fatherly connection, I had minimal contact with him as I grew older. I made a conscious choice in my early thirties not to include him in my life.

When my mother brought me to upstate New York, my grandmother, mortified that I had lived three years without being baptized, took me to a priest to rectify the situation. Soon after our arrival, my mother got drunk, took me for a drive on a windy back road and attempted suicide. We both lived, but the judge ordered my mother into a state mental hospital for two years. Feeling unwanted and unloved, I was shuttled back and forth between her parents' and her oldest brother's homes until I finished kindergarten.

The only mention of God in our family occurred on Easter, Christmas, or when someone died. My grandmother was raised in a legalistic religion, but my grandfather had disdain for God and His church. My first beliefs saw God as distant and uninterested—too busy for the likes of me. Both my grandparents were alcoholics and could be mean without provocation. I thought it was my fault, because I ruined their plans for retirement. I learned to watch the moods of adults and adjust my behavior.

At five, I was late getting home from the bus after school, and my grandmother was angry. She got a belt or a branch from a tree. I can't remember. She told me to take off all my clothes and get on the kitchen table for a big surprise. What five-year-old doesn't like surprises? I desperately wanted to earn my grandmother's affections, so I did as I was told. I was beaten on my back, buttocks, and genitals while she screamed at me to never scare her again.

I didn't. I did everything I could to be perfect. Anxiety in the form of stomach aches and headaches began around that time and manifest to this day when stress creeps in.

My grandfather verbally abused me. He'd joke about the mosquito bites I had for breasts and how I'd better hope they'd grow, or I would never find a husband. Occasionally, my mother came for visitations. "Tell your mother what I taught you," he said. "What are you going to be when you grow up, Alynda?"

"I will be a whore just like my mother," I said—the reply that he had taught me.

The taunting caused me to believe that something about me was damaged. I thought I wasn't good enough the way I was. His calloused words, my grandmother's anger and abuse, and my mother's absence all set the stage for multiple incidents of sexual abuse.

Eventually, the hospital released my mother. My grandmother drove me to her apartment and left me there. In a strange town alone with this woman I hardly knew, I was scared and lonely. My mother, still depressed, used alcohol and drugs to numb her pain, so I was often with babysitters or left alone. One teenage babysitter sexually abused me. Older children also wanted to play this game. I vacillated between believing this was normal and knowing, deep down, it was secretly making me a bad girl. I lost track of how many times these games were played and with how many children—girls and boys alike.

After a few years, my mother and I moved to Oklahoma to be near my father's family. My granny, the first person to mention the love of Jesus, took me to the First Baptist Church, where I heard "Amazing Grace" sung for the first time. Tears welled up in my eyes, and hair rose on my arms. The song was about me. I was the wretch. I prayed that the Jesus of that song would love me too. This was when I first found Christ, but I had little of His influence in my day-to-day life. I didn't know how to walk with Him.

When I was in the sixth grade, my mother met another man, Mike, who became my stepfather. A few months later, we moved to Dallas. Moving was nothing new. We lived in over twenty trailers, apartments, and rental homes, and I attended ten schools before graduating from high school. Mike left pornography around the trailer for me to see. When I broke rules, he spanked my bare buttocks while he wore only a robe with no undergarments.

Over thirty-five years later, I have conflicted feelings about my stepfather. He showed fatherly love by seeming to be the first person to care about my education and dreams. He also subjected me to drugs and pornography. In my teens, he sexually assaulted me. I have tried to rationalize his behaviors, but actually he was a man desperately in need of a Savior. Tragically, during my twenties, his life ended in a drug overdose, and I never knew if he found the Lord.

The feelings of dirtiness never left me, and I classified the good girls from school and church as better than me. I wanted Jesus to love me, but I thought I was too dirty for His good, clean love. I was too young to understand that anything can be cleansed through Christ. In Ezekiel 36:25, the Lord tells us, "I will sprinkle clean water on you, and you will be clean; I will cleanse you from all your impurities and from all your idols."

An older boy pursued me. He was almost eighteen. I had just turned fourteen. I thought it was love. He broke up with me two weeks later. This led to my promiscuity. What did it matter? It was all I had to give, so why not do it?

Living in poverty, my parents couldn't afford an apartment without roommates. Some of the men my parents allowed to live with us added to the number of my perpetrators. I gave up on the idea that I might be valuable.

In January of my ninth-grade year, Mom and I found ourselves homeless. I slept on a friend's couch, and she slept in our car. She met a stranger in a bar, who offered to let us live with him in his one-bedroom apartment if I slept in the bed with him. She agreed.

Charlie bought me gifts. He drove me to school and took me out to eat. Slowly over a month or two, he isolated me from everyone else. At night, he touched me when I was asleep, then told me in the morning that I had just dreamed it. This escalated into a nightly experience that convinced me that I was, indeed, the dirty, shameful girl I had always thought I was. To keep me in line, he alternately used generous gifts and threats of hurting my mother. I grew to believe myself complicit in these acts, as if I wanted them to happen, as if they were as much my fault as his. They were just one more secret for me to keep. Throughout the rest of my teens and early twenties, there were more abusers. My boundaries were nonexistent.

At seventeen, I moved out on my own with a boyfriend and worked at a topless club. I used drugs and alcohol. I felt in control as I'd never felt before. Of course, that was a false sense of control. I drank to get the nerve to dance. I did drugs for courage to talk to the men in the club. I didn't care what happened. Being groped, assaulted, and called a whore by strangers was what I deserved. It was my worth. Or so I thought.

After finding out I was pregnant, I married a man who worked in the club. Physically and mentally abusive, he convinced me to work in pornography with him. But when I gave birth to my daughter, things needed to change. I looked at her face and decided I didn't want that life for her. Yet I didn't know how to make better decisions. I felt trapped, unable to see any way to a better life.

I'd take a step in the right direction, but self-protection, fear of the unknown, and a lack of understanding of Christ's love always led me back to where I shouldn't be. By the time I was twenty-four, I had married and divorced twice, with several other dysfunctional relationships. I tried to feed my God-shaped hole with relationships, sex, education, money, shopping, and prescription drugs. I tried anything that would dull the pain, but none of it worked. None of it did what I needed, because none of it was God. The Lord shows us in John 15:5, "I am the vine; you are the branches. If you remain in me and I in you, you will bear much fruit; apart from me you can do nothing."

I dabbled in the Christian life by sporadically attending church, offering a feeble prayer or two, and glancing through the books of the Bible. I liked the idea, but I was such a slave to my flesh. I had little desire to walk the narrow path. I chose not to take responsibility for the choices I had made in the wake of my abuse. I was life's victim, and I wore my victim mentality on my sleeve. I still believed I was too tarnished for God's goodness and forgiveness.

I met a man who said he loved Jesus, and I put my faith in him while professing to put my faith in Christ. We had a rocky start to our relationship, but we married six years later. He adopted my daughter, and we had two more beautiful daughters. We occasionally attended church near our home. When life was tough, we attended church for a few weeks. As soon as we believed we had control over our struggles, we fell away again.

I was addicted to prescription pain medication for debilitating migraines. The drugs took the edge off the headaches and reduced the effects of night terrors and flashbacks that I had secretly experienced since my early teens. I was hidden inside myself. I believed any authenticity or transparency would immediately push far away anyone who professed to love me. I thought if I could act like a normal mother and wife, I would become one.

In January 2016, my life imploded. I'd tried everything I could find to "fix me." During the day, I looked like I had it together. I was a stay-at-home mother who partially homeschooled the girls. I baked muffins, volunteered at school, and attempted the Pinterest lifestyle that overwhelms so many women. At night, I could no longer hide my nightmares and flashbacks from my husband. I either didn't sleep or woke up screaming from memories of abuse.

My anxiety intensified, and leaving my home terrified me. I hovered over my daughters in the fear they would fall or get hurt. Then I would have failed as their mother. My abuse engulfed my life. I wanted to die. I believed my husband and kids would be better in a world that didn't include me. I was a burden to everyone who knew me, and it would be better if I no longer existed.

Due to my suicidal ideation and crippling anxiety, I checked myself into a faith-based psychiatric facility, where I came face-to-face with the God of the universe. I clung to Psalm 34:18: "The Lord is close to the brokenhearted and saves those who are crushed in spirit." I was both. At the end of myself, I found a loving and merciful God.

While in the hospital, the outtake nurse told me about "Shelter," a sexual abuse recovery program at Watermark Church. After leaving the hospital and attending a month-long outpatient program, I walked through the doors of "Shelter." I sat far away from everyone and cried the entire time. When a woman gave her testimony, I felt a surge of hope. Parts of her story were like mine. I began the process of recovery right away and dove in. It was scary but also freeing to know there was a safe place, a sisterhood of other women seeking the same healing that I desperately wanted through our Father in Heaven.

I made friends—no, not friends—sisters. Several of us bonded in a support circle as we each started our healing process. Recovery was hard work, with each week uncovering lies we'd been told and told ourselves. I cried many weeks, but they were tears of relief over the realization that, although God allowed my abuse to occur, He never wanted that life for me.

Psalm 56:8 tells us, "Record my misery; list my tears on your scroll—are they not in your record?" I envisioned a large bottle that God had carefully tended for the past forty-four years. I was trying to be my children's savior instead of entrusting them to Christ. I had believed my abuse was my fault, but I now knew I had no ability to consent. My perpetrators bore the burden for those sins. I learned that forgiveness was not only possible, but the Lord required it of me. I thought I had to forgive myself, but I learned when I surrendered my life to Christ that He had already forgiven me. There was nothing else for me to do.

I was free. I was being transformed. 2 Corinthians 5:17 says, "Therefore, if anyone is in Christ, the new creation has come: the old has gone, the new is here!" When I finished "Shelter," I wanted to join leadership to help others experience the healing I'd experienced. My leader urged me to first attend "Re:Generation," Watermark's twelve-step recovery program. I didn't think I needed to attend, but after only a few weeks, I realized I needed to work through the choices I'd made since my abuse.

My life is not "all better" now. I still struggle. I can still fall back into old patterns if I am not aware that I have only one Savior who is sufficient, who loves me and wants good for me every day. My identity is in Christ alone. When I falter, I have women of God who walk alongside me, to help steer me back onto the right path. My husband and I attended Watermark's marriage ministry, "Re-Engage," to learn how to center our marriage around Christ instead of each other. God never promises to take our pasts away or undo what has been done to us, but He promises to repay those years. He promises He will redeem us from the pit and renew our youth like the eagles. I am so thankful for a Savior who meets me in my brokenness and brings light into my darkness.

Three years ago, I wouldn't speak the words molestation, rape, and sexual abuse above a whisper, but I now willingly talk about how God has transformed my life through my abuse. Anxiety doesn't control me anymore. I know my feelings are real, but they are not always reliable. I know there is an enemy who wants to pull me away from the goodness of God, but I have my armor on. I no longer live in darkness, because now, I know hope.

Alynda Long *is a writer, blogger, editor, and redeemed survivor of sexual abuse. A lay leader in a recovery ministry, she loves helping other women walk through their own journey of recovery through Christ. Alynda is Founder and Editor of Faith Beyond Fear, a site dedicated to sharing believers' experiences of reaching beyond fear into their faith in Christ. She also contributes to the website, A Wife Like Me. She thrives on Jesus, coffee, books, chocolate, and friendships.*

AlyndaLong.com
AlyndaLong@gmail.com.

Thoughts to Ponder

from Hope in the Darkness

1. Nothing and no one is too far gone for Christ.

2. He will restore the years the locusts have eaten, if we have willing and trusting hearts and minds.

3. Although it often feels like it, we are never alone.

How has God restored the years the locusts have eaten in your life?

I will repay you for the years the locusts have eaten. — *Joel 2:25*

Dead End

by Mike Branch

Another late night on a lonely road, and there was that voice again, *Kill yourself.* The darkness outside was no match for the darkness inside me. Guilt brought every hope to a dead end. Perhaps you've been on that road before, or you find yourself there now. Here's how my journey from despair to freedom unfolded—and the marvelous, unexpected way God showed me that He already knew the end from the beginning.

It was November 1976. The rumbling lullaby of a short-block-350 motor kept coaxing my eyelids downward on the highway. My 1955 Chevy pickup and I had made this trip together countless times. So I was very familiar, this stretch of Interstate 35 between Austin (University of Texas) and Fort Worth (girlfriend and home). A familiar road, and that familiar suggestion to escape this life.

Kill yourself.

I cranked up the eight-track tape player to drown out the voice. I looked for distractions, running my hands across the truck's burnt-orange bench seat. No relief there. I hated that fresh padding and perfect stitching. I glanced up at the new headliner, another tangible reminder of my guilt. One by one, the miles passed.

Just drive across the median. Hit a car.

The voice kept nagging, more insistent than the doleful tunes of Willie Nelson. I stroked the finely finished wood handle of the fancy chrome floor-shifter. It gave me chills. Oncoming headlights gleamed off the flawless orange paint of the hood. My gloom intensified.

You're in too deep. That's what shame feels like.

The voice was right. Its accusations heaped up day after day, night after night, until I could no longer see around them. How did I ever get into this mess? Hopeless. Endless. Numbing. It was true of this drive, true of my life. I hated that truck.

Have you ever felt that way? Have you ever come to the end of your rope? Maybe you are there right now. Hang on. There's hope. We cannot come to repentance unless God produces in us a grief for who and what we are as sinners. His redeeming work begins with the gift of eyes to see our desperate need. "Godly sorrow brings repentance that leads to salvation and leaves no regret, but worldly sorrow brings death" (2 Corinthians 7:10). I didn't always hate my truck. In fact, I started out loving her more than anything.

In high school, we kids shared one of the family's cars. In my first year of college, I bummed rides. I was a sophomore before I got wheels of my own. All I could afford was a twenty-year-old rusty pickup that said "For Sale, $250" in the back window. Of course, it needed a little work, but it was mine. It was love at first sight.

One summer, I worked for a soft drink company where family friends owned and managed the operation. Every day I drove a fully-loaded truck to the company's parking lot and sold cases of soft drinks to church groups, convenience store owners, and anybody else authorized to buy wholesale.

A guy who sits in a parking lot all day has time to think. What he thinks about says a lot about what his heart treasures most. This guy thought a lot about his truck, strategically parked where he could see it all day. This guy thought, *That truck could use some paint. That truck could use better suspension. That truck could use . . .*

You could say I idolized that truck. What I did that summer proves I did. It worked like this: Sometimes people needed more soft drinks than I had with me in the parking lot, especially around holidays. So I retrieved more cases from the warehouse and added them to my beginning inventory. At day's end, I reconciled the accounting like any truck route driver, matching up dollars received and inventory sold.

One day, I failed to mark some added cases to my beginning inventory. When you do that, you come up with extra cash at day's end. At first, my conscience hurt to stick that cash into my pocket, but it hurt less the next day, and the next. Soon it became no problem to pay for work done on my idol with thousands of dollars stolen from work. Bodywork, paint, interior, motor, transmission. It was looking good.

I went to church. I read my Bible. I prayed. But my heart was out in the truck. Pride. Self-sufficiency. Insatiable desires for more, no matter the cost.

Bad heart-habits are hard to break, even if you want to. In Austin, I landed a job as cashier at a retailer. I shared the register with others, but it was still possible to slip a few dollars out of the tray once in a while. Then I came back to Fort Worth and spent another summer selling soft drinks in the parking lot.

That's when that destructive voice of conscience began—the one that kept nagging me on lonely, late-night drives. I was driving forward, but at the same time, I was at a dead end. I came home every other weekend, so the voice was plenty familiar by Thanksgiving 1976. On that holiday drive, the voice was more insistent than ever.

It's hopeless. Kill yourself.

Have you ever wondered how you got trapped in some mess? Do you wonder how you fell for Satan's lie, which has become your prison? It's a hard, scary place to be. The thing you loved now locks you up and rules you. Maybe it's your hidden dungeon of pornography, jealousy, seething anger, or something else that only you know. Satan's whispers lead us to destruction—on paths that take us away from our only true Source of Life, Jesus Christ. The good news is that our Source of Life pursues us. Our hopelessness is visible only by the light God shines, and our freedom is possible only through the blood Jesus shed.

By God's grace and will, I kept driving that night. God protected me from the voice, and I made the journey to Fort Worth safely.

But the next night, while I was watching TV at my girlfriend's house, a spiritual showdown occurred. God had seen enough of my divided heart. In His time and His way, He finally crushed me with conviction, so much so that I collapsed into heaps of uncontrollable sobbing. God's sorrow became my sorrow. The story could no longer hide. Choking out the truth to my bewildered girlfriend took a long time.

Confession. It was the only exit, and God caused my hardened heart to open. He drove me to confess to my shocked parents. I confessed to my dumbfounded pastor. I confessed to my astonished employers, who mercifully pressed no charges. But most of all, I confessed to God—whose holiness stood in stark contrast to my own stained soul.

By God's grace, He moved my heart to repentance—not to escape the worldly consequences of my sin, but because it was God's way of tearing down the bars that held me captive. He lanced a deep wound and drained out the ugly. He shined light into my darkest recesses. As a result, He did the impossible: He restored

28

my fellowship with Him.

There were painful consequences, of course. I left the Austin college scene and returned to Fort Worth. I left the apartment life to live at home. I sold the truck. I licked my wounded reputation. And most of what I earned during the next several years went to my former employers.

But the voice was gone. In its place was that peace that defies understanding (Philippians 4:7). Coming home felt so good. I understood how that prodigal son felt in Luke 15. My parents did too.

Conviction, repentance, confession, and restoration. That cycle is God's precious gift for believers, the only exit from the sinful places our hearts can take us. That cycle is possible only because Jesus exchanges His righteousness for each sinner who comes to beg Him for it.

You may find yourself thinking your heart is too deeply off course for this to apply. You may feel ashamed of some things. You may hear an accuser's voice suggesting you are hopeless. Don't let these things hold you captive. Christ came to set you free. Take the exit that only He provides. Thank Him for revealing your heart to you. He didn't have to, you know.

Have you ever felt the sudden release of sin's unbearable accusations? Praise God! Only Jesus' sacrifice makes it possible. Only God's mercy makes it applicable. Confession and forgiveness. It's the best feeling in the world, because it is God's voice saying, "Welcome home."

"Therefore, there is now no condemnation for those who are in Christ Jesus, because through Christ Jesus the law of the Spirit who gives life has set you free from the law of sin and death" (Romans 8:1–2).

This is my true story about one of the darkest periods in my life. Faced with guilt for stealing thousands of dollars, I finally collapsed under the pressure. God compelled me to turn myself in—to my girlfriend, my parents, my pastor, and the companies I stole from. I lost my job, my reputation, and my independence. It took several years to repay the companies while I lived at home and finished college.

But that's not the whole story.

Two weeks before my story reached its climax, a middle-aged

couple slipped quietly into the pews at a Fort Worth church. The surroundings were familiar. They had worshiped there for more than twenty-five years. They had faithfully raised a family there, bringing two sons and a daughter through Sunday school.

This particular night, a special service for healing was in progress. The couple was not sick. Perhaps they came with his aging father in mind. Like others in the congregation, they were asked to write their healing need on a 3x5 card.

When it was their turn, the couple rose from their pew and walked up the aisle to an area in front of the altar. They handed their card to the two pastors, who laid hands on their heads and prayed for the healing they desired.

As the pastors read the card, they noticed that the couple was not praying for a physical healing of any sort. The card simply said, "For our family."

The words of their prayer for the healing of a family that night echoed off the marble floor, resonating past the richly carved wood of the church and into the highest reaches of the sanctuary and beyond. It mirrored their own ongoing, urgent prayers, casting their cares on the only source of redemption, hope, and change.

Mom and Dad were there that night. My parents were the couple who prayed for a healed family, even as my soul was mired in a secret and dark prison they didn't know about. As they drove home, their prayer lay before God's heart and worked its way into His sovereign plan.

Two weeks later, I was healed and came home. I was set free. I was restored to my family and to God. Cleansed of my guilt, I was given a clean bill of spiritual health by God Himself.

Once buried in despair, I was suddenly resurrected in hope. As painful as it was, I rejoiced then and I rejoice today that God lifted my life out of quicksand and placed it again on a solid rock.

If you still see Jesus only as an example of good deeds and a lover of whatever path you choose, if you believe in God only to satisfy your selfish longings, I pray He opens your eyes. That "Jesus" has no power to deal with your sins when your earthly days are spent and you are confronted with God's holiness.

Have you run to Jesus as Son of God but still fall prey to Satan's deceitful whispers? Jesus exchanged His life for yours on the cross so His righteous life could become your life. I pray that God brings you to that same crushing moment I experienced. May He bring you to repentance and the liberty you yearn for.

If you feel like you are at a dead end and have simply "lost your first love" for Christ, as John reports of one church in Revelation 2, I pray God will rekindle your affections for Him. May your passion for Christ and His ways burst into flames, consuming every other passion that hinders you.

Michael Branch—*One Christmas morning in elementary school, Mike was surprised with a gift he never thought to ask for but loved at first sight. It was an old mechanical typewriter that inspired a job in newspapers, a career in magazines, and work in marketing and copywriting. He and his wife, Sherry, have four children and are expecting their thirteenth grandchild. Last year, he published his first book,* True Stories to Remind You of Heaven When Life Hurts Like Hell, *available at **PicklePerfectPublishing.com.***

Thoughts to Ponder
from Dead End

1. We can be imprisoned by the lies the enemy whispers to us.

2. Repentance leads to liberty.

3. God can bring the prodigal child home.

Do you need to repent of any hidden sin in your life?

For he has rescued us from the dominion of darkness and brought us into the kingdom of the Son he loves, in whom we have redemption, the forgiveness of sins. — Colossians 1:13–14

More than We Could Handle

by DeLayne Haga

In July 2010, the love of my life was diagnosed with inoperable stage IV lung cancer that had metastasized to his brain. We were stunned—*he had never smoked.*

Within three months of his diagnosis, the mass in my husband's lung almost tripled in size to thirteen centimeters—almost half the length of a ruler—before we found a successful regimen to shrink the cancer. The doctor originally gave Chris a prognosis of six months. Instead, he lived six *years*. He was officially declared to have "no evidence of disease" on three separate occasions.

When we found out Chris had tumors in his lung, I had never heard of anyone surviving stage IV lung cancer for long, and I had no hope that the love of my life would. But God had a plan for the trial we faced.

Chris prayed a simple prayer for God to place the right people in the right place at the right time. And so many times, God answered. The Lord knew who and what we needed before we did. And He was faithful to meet our needs, though not always in the way we expected.

We went out to eat a couple nights after Chris was diagnosed. As we approached the restaurant, an obese man was smoking near the door. Unexpected anger and resentment toward that individual hit us hard. *He* deserved lung cancer, not Chris. That anger was short-lived, because God quickly opened our minds. We realized that no one deserves the disease. We're no better than anyone else in God's eyes.

Instead of asking, "Why me?" my husband then asked, "Why not me?" That turning point helped us understand there must be some reason Chris was chosen to have lung cancer. This was all part of God's plan for our lives. Maybe it was a test. Was our faith genuine? Would we love or reject Him?

After the diagnosis, we attended church. The title of the sermon that morning was "Healed of a Lengthy Affliction." As Chris read the bulletin, he heard a voice out of nowhere say, *It will be a long, hard battle, but you will be healed.*

When we started the cancer journey, we developed a sense of

peace about the situation. Maybe we were just being naïve, but we felt God was in control. Chris described it as being in the eye of the storm. Where we were at that time was calm. If we kept our focus on Jesus, we didn't see the storm building around us. But as soon as we tried to look too far ahead, we saw the rolling storm clouds and became scared with the uncertainty of it all.

After the diagnostic tests at MD Anderson Cancer Center in Houston, we learned that the cancer had spread in the few weeks since diagnosis.

Gamma Knife radiation on the brain tumor in September was successful. Chris was scheduled in October to start standard chemotherapy near our home in the Dallas area. But three days prior, he ended up in the hospital at MD Anderson with recurring pneumonia. The oncologist recognized that the tumor was blocking his airway and preventing the antibiotics from clearing up his pneumonia. Undergoing chemo while he was battling pneumonia could have damaged his immune system and been fatal. This doctor at MD Anderson quickly changed the treatment plan. The doctor also had the lung biopsy tested for a rare gene mutation. Chris did indeed have that mutation, and a clinical trial was available to treat the cancer. Before he could qualify to get into the clinical trial, he had fifteen rounds of radiation to shrink the tumor and then was required to have three rounds of standard chemo and still show progression of disease. By the time he finished radiation, he was thirty pounds below his normal weight and looked like death warmed over.

I need to confess something: I used to open my Bible only on Sundays. Over the years, I had tried reading through it many times but lost interest, because I was reading it as merely a history book instead of God's message to mankind.

We were driving to Houston, a captive audience listening to four preachers on our favorite Christian radio station. Each pastor's sermon was on the importance of reading your Bible first thing in the morning.

"Okay, God," I shouted. "I got the message."

His voice may not have been audible, but His message came through loud and clear. I needed to deepen my knowledge and strengthen my spiritual walk. I made a commitment to read the Bible every day. For as long as I could remember, my husband had been faithful to daily read his Bible. It's sad to think it took a cancer diagnosis to get me to follow his example.

The book of Job reminded me that Christians were never promised an easy life. Even if my husband didn't survive, God was in control, and it would be part of His plan. He would take care of me.

Doubts still occasionally slithered into my thoughts, gnawing at my belief that God would heal Chris. Concentration on any scripture was challenging. In the front and back covers of my Bible, I listed everything I was thankful the Lord had provided. In the dark hours filled with fear and worry, I read over the list and made a conscious effort to thank the Lord for everything. The mental transformation that takes place when your heart exudes gratitude is amazing.

Chris started chemo in December 2010. Although the radiation and chemo were doing their job to shrink the cancer, a suspicious spot in his liver appeared, so Chris was switched to another chemo. This new regimen was also working to kill the cancer, but it put him into the hospital with an almost non-existent immune system—which that type of chemo rarely causes. This turned out to be a positive thing. Although the chemo was working, it prevented him from qualifying for the clinical trial. But the adverse reaction of this chemo, causing a compromised immune system, allowed him to get into the clinical trial for a drug that showed promising results. Only God could have orchestrated such an intricate plan. Things were looking up, and so were we.

Chris's health continued to improve quickly. We reflected on all we had been through and how we had survived. There's a popular saying: "God never gives you more than you can handle." We were finding this was far from the truth. If we could handle this on our own, there wouldn't be any need for the numerous people who rallied around us with support and food. If God didn't give us more than we could handle, then what role was there for Jesus? If we were able to fix this on our own, exactly when would we learn to depend on Him? We couldn't handle cancer by ourselves, but we didn't have to.

In May 2011, Chris realized he was breathing easier. He heard the same voice that had told him he was in for a long, hard battle. But this time, the voice said, *The tumor is gone.*

A week later, his scans verified that there was no evidence of disease. You'd think we'd be jumping up and down with joy, but we weren't surprised. A voice had already leaked the news.

In the world of advanced lung cancer treatment, "no evidence of disease" is as good as it gets. He would always be considered to have at least stable stage IV lung cancer and would need to be in active treatment for the rest of his life. Tiny diseased cells tend to hide, and advanced lung cancer almost always comes back. The doctor said that due to radiation fibrosis, Chris's lung would probably never reinflate. "Performing radiation on any portion of the lung is essentially like removing that portion of the lung," he said.

"We may have found the limits of medicine," Chris said, "but there's no limit to what God can do." His faith was stronger than mine.

While I agreed that God *could* do such a miracle, deep down I had my doubts that He *would*. I didn't tell Chris my doubts. I couldn't dash his hopes. Hope was the one thing that kept him going.

After he went from death's door with stage IV lung cancer to no evidence of disease, I realized that God does His most magnificent work when the situation is impossible from a human viewpoint.

Chris was living a normal life again, and we went to Hawaii in September 2011 for vacation.

The cancer treatment caused severe osteoporosis, requiring two back surgeries for five fractures in his spine. He developed pneumonia again, and a doctor drained almost two liters of fluid from around his lung. We learned during this time that cancer is not just a physical and emotional battle, but it is also a spiritual battle. At times, Chris had to force himself to read the Bible and pray, because it seemed God wasn't listening.

One morning, my husband pleaded with God to show him some mercy. Suddenly, the song "It Is Well with My Soul" was playing in his head. He got mad at God and said that under no circumstances was any of this "well with his soul." He tried to recall some memory verses, and the only verse that came to his mind was, "My God, my God, why have You forsaken Me?"

Even though we had experienced what seemed like setback after setback, we were slowly realizing that this was part of God's perfect plan. Sometimes we must experience a low point in our lives to show God's power.

Chris's health improved again, and he was able to walk a mile without getting out of breath. He decided he could finally make it to church for the first time in several months, but he had difficulty breathing as he was getting ready. He wondered why he was having such a problem. His little voice told him, *Satan doesn't want you in church*. Determined not to let Satan get the upper hand, Chris made it to church, although each step got harder. The sermon was from Psalm 139 about how God formed us and knew before we were born the number of our days. Satan apparently didn't want us to be encouraged. He didn't want Chris back in the game. But thanks to Jesus, Satan had lost the match.

In January 2013, we learned that the cancer had returned. I sat by Chris's bedside in the recovery room after a lung biopsy and researched clinical trials. We wanted the trial for what I will call Drug A, which was showing an 80 percent positive response to the drug, but all the Phase I trials were closed, and Phase II hadn't opened yet. The second most effective drug was Drug B, which was available at a small clinic we had never heard of in Fayetteville, Arkansas. Chris's oncologist made the referral, and the research assistant from Arkansas called. The trial for Drug B had just closed, but a Phase II trial for Drug A had just opened. Chris was the first patient in the United States to get into the trial.

What are the odds? Less than an hour before meeting with the oncologist in Houston, I found the only place in the United States that had opened the trial we wanted. In a tiny, unknown clinic— just when Chris's current treatment had stopped working, God had closed one door and opened the door to a better opportunity as He navigated our course.

Chris's health rapidly improved on the new drug, and he was successfully pursuing his dream to become cancer-free. While he was pursuing *his* dream, our older son, Chad, was pursing his own dream of being a professional cyclist. He made it to the pro level, but we had never watched him race in person as a pro.

When God opened the door to the study in Arkansas, we couldn't figure out why, of all the clinics in the United States that were trying to open the trial, this little clinic was first. When Chad found out that his team would be racing in Fayetteville the week of

Chris's exam, we extended our stay and saw Chad get his first major win as a pro. We knew then that God had allowed Chris's and Chad's dreams to intersect. Chad was a pro cyclist, and Chris was healed of cancer again.

A year later, the cancer returned. Chris entered a clinical trial for Drug C at MD Anderson. He had a severe reaction to the drug and had to stop taking it for almost two weeks. After eight weeks in the trial, scans showed that the cancer had progressed, so he had to leave the trial.

Chris got into a fourth clinical trial in November 2014, and by March 2015, he had no evidence of disease for the third time. My husband was a living miracle. But all the side-effects of the treatment caused a lot of anxiety as his weekly treatment day grew closer. He got physically sick at the *thought* of getting another round of chemo, so the oncologist reduced his dosage and let him take a two-week break.

A month later, Chris began coughing, and his breathing exercises showed a rapid decline. The doctor agreed with Chris that we didn't need a CT scan to tell us the cancer was back. He dropped out of the clinical trial and switched to a standard chemo, since we were out of options for clinical trials.

Chris felt sure the end was coming soon, and he wouldn't live long enough to start chemo the following week. We had some heart-wrenching talks that week, and he updated his funeral directives for me.

I prayed, *Lord, don't let this be the end. I'm not ready to let him go.*

Unable to sleep, I remembered David's war cry in 1 Samuel: "The battle is the Lord's." God was in control. My fears calmed, and I found peace in thinking about the good things and miracles that God had done. Reminded that our problems are God's opportunities to show His power, I fell asleep, praying for another miracle.

Fatigue was a major side-effect of the chemo. With all the other side-effects, Chris suffered from depression. One day, his nurse returned my phone call while I was at the grocery store. She asked how he was doing. That's all it took to leave me standing in a puddle of tears in the middle of the store. She suggested he see a palliative care doctor to help him improve his appetite, mood, nausea, depression, and insomnia.

Having witnessed healing numerous times already, we knew God could heal Chris. But we were losing confidence that this was His plan. We were depending on others to pray for us, to trust that God would restore Chris's health once more. What we were experiencing made it difficult to see what God saw for the future.

God continued to put the right person in the right place at the right time. With the help of one prescription from the palliative care doctor, Chris's health and outlook on life made a dramatic improvement within just one week. Scans showed that the chemo was working. A small part of his collapsed lung reinflated a little. The doctor was surprised at the resilience of Chris's lung. He said, "A lung doesn't normally open back up when it's been collapsed for as long as yours has, especially when it's due to radiation fibrosis."

We counted that as a small miracle. Chris's faith had moved a mountain.

By January 2016, the chemo had taken a toll on Chris's kidneys, and he had to stop cancer treatment. A kidney biopsy showed he had developed a rare condition, which required experimental treatment. That month, he felt better than he had in a long time, since he was off all cancer treatment and medications to deal with side-effects. But in mid-May, breathing difficulties were getting worse by the day. He had dietary and fluid restrictions because of his kidneys, and he felt that God was taking away his food, water, and breath. We were out of treatment options, and he had lost his quality of life.

Chris was God's gift to me, but I knew He would want Chris back some day. I was now ready for that time, and we prayed for God to take him home. We made final preparations for his funeral, and he signed a "Do Not Resuscitate" form.

Chris wasn't afraid of death, but he was terrified of prolonged suffering and suffocating. I was also scared of how he might suffer. Numerous scenarios ran through my mind. None of them occurred. I would have saved myself a lot of heartache if I had remembered, there's no need to worry—God's got everything under His control. I'll admit, it was easier to worry than to turn to prayer.

Chad was on his summer break from racing and drove from Colorado with his fiancée to be with his dad in the hospital. Our younger son, Shane, drove twenty-five hours from Mexico, where he had been doing missionary work. Chris was in a coma, and the nurse expected him to pass that night. But he lingered through the night, breathing shallow, just four times a minute. We decided to take turns holding vigil.

While the others were sleeping, I suddenly felt all alone in the dark room. But I wasn't. A small, quivering smile crept onto my face. I prayed, *Thank You for being here for me, Lord. I couldn't do this without Your love carrying me through these darkest moments.* Tears of both joy and sorrow flowed down my face as I realized that Jesus would be taking the place of my husband.

Chris passed away peacefully at seven o'clock on Saturday morning, June 25, 2016. Assured of Chris's salvation and that he was now with the Lord, I was also at peace in my heart. He faced death courageously, knowing he would soon be spending eternity in Heaven. He fought for his life to the end. Although it wasn't the healing on Earth that we prayed for, he kept his faith.

I finally understood why God prolonged the last day of Chris's life. God had a plan for His timetable. It wasn't a coincidence that Chris passed on Saturday, 6/25, at exactly seven o'clock. God knew all along that nothing else would give me such peace about my husband's passing as that date and precise time. You see, Chris loved to ride his bicycle. His favorite time to ride was early Saturday mornings at sunrise. He liked to be out the door by seven o'clock. And his favorite Bible verse was Matthew 6:25, which tells us not to worry. He had the ride of his life that morning.

I don't know how many times over the years I heard Chris tell me, "You worry too much." Even through his death, Chris was still reminding me, "Do not worry. God is in control."

DeLayne Haga is the author of His Love Carries Me *and published her husband's companion book,* Cancer on Two Wheels *posthumously. Married for thirty-two years, Chris and DeLayne raised two sons. DeLayne resides in McKinney, Texas, and owns a secretarial/bookkeeping business. She is a member of Stonebriar Community Church in Frisco, Texas. For information about Chris and DeLayne's books, visit* HagaBooksofFaith.com *or send an email to* HagaBooksofFaith@gmail.com.

Thoughts to Ponder
from More than We Could Handle

1. Our problems are opportunities for God to show His power.

2. In times of tribulation, don't close your Bible—open it.

3. Pray for the right people in the right place at the right time.

What are you worrying about that God can handle for you?

Therefore I tell you, do not worry about your life, what you will eat or drink; or about your body, what you will wear. Is not life more than food, and the body more than clothes? — Matthew 6:25

Whispers of Love
by Deanna L. Martin

Do you remember when, as a child, you dreamed what your life would be like? A girl might dream something like the last scene of *Pretty Woman*, when Richard Gere becomes Julia Robert's Prince Charming, rescues her, and takes her away to love her forever. Or maybe you, like me, imagined yourself in the perfect little house, with the perfect spouse, and the most perfect little children.

As the oldest of four girls, I dreamed of being a wife and mom, just like my mother was. I imagined marrying a handsome, romantic guy who loved me no matter what. He worshipped me and wanted to please me in every way. I would be a happy, fulfilled, and appreciated wife, and my husband and I would have a wonderful, loving marriage, living happily ever after as we drove off into the sunset of our lives.

As my dear dad always said, "It sounds easy when you say it fast."

In my eighth-grade year, our family moved to the country. A few years later, I dated John, the boy next door. I fell in love with a long-haired hippie. (Hey, it was the 70s.) He seemed a bit dangerous and was from a world completely different from my sheltered world. I was from a family of love and trust. My parents still loved each other and were happily married. I was the "apple of my daddy's eye" and could do anything I set out to accomplish. On the other hand, John was from a family laden with divorce and heartache. He found it hard to trust, but I believed my love could change all that.

John joined the service, and we married on his first two-week leave. We moved from Texas to Illinois for his tech training. It was my first time away from home without my family. Embarrassingly enough, I cried that first night on the road. I missed my mom. We settled into a little shack with roaches everywhere and tape on the walls and furniture. This was our first home, and we started our daily routine.

Just a month later, John, my prince, told me he had made a mistake in marrying me. He said he didn't really love me and admitted that he paced back and forth in indecision the day before our wedding, knowing it would be a mistake to go through with it. His mom even advised him not to marry me.

I was shattered. There was no going back, because I didn't believe in divorce. No one in my family had ever divorced. I cried the first of many tears. To John's credit, he decided to stay and make a go of it.

Through the years, we had good times and bad. In our own personal roller coaster over the next decade, John and I often talked in bed. The conversation went something like this:

"Are you happy?" he asked.

"Umm . . . yes. Aren't you?"

His reply always surprised me. "No, I am miserable."

My world rocked again and again. Try as I might, I could not make it better. Being the oldest child, I believed I could accomplish anything on which I set my mind, but I couldn't *make* my husband love me.

After twelve years and three sons, I found myself in a terribly rocky marriage with a man who still said he *never* loved me. Where was the dream? What happened to my Prince Charming?

When John was offered a job in California, he left alone, with the understanding that the boys and I would follow him after the school year ended. However, when the time came for us join him, he couldn't make up his mind whether he wanted us to move. Eventually, he decided to stay married to me, so the boys and I moved to California. Though my dad tried hard to dissuade me, I felt I had to go. After all, John was my husband, and my place was with him. However, since nothing had really changed between us, it should not have come as a surprise when, only two weeks after we arrived, he told me he had "made a mistake in bringing us out." He just didn't love me.

I ran from our bedroom to the living room, crying bitter, heart-wrenching tears. Here I was, a thousand miles from home and thinking, *Now what? What am I going to do?* I felt so alone.

Again, life went on. Our roller-coaster continued in our small two-bedroom apartment with rented furniture and mattresses on the floor. I found a job and worked while our boys were in school. After eight months, our youngest son, Zachary, became severely ill.

My husband and I took Zachary to the doctor, where tests indicated spinal meningitis. "Take him immediately to the ER," they said. "Don't have an accident on the way, and don't take any wrong turns." Zach was in a coma. Terrified, I called my parents in Texas. By evening, my mom arrived to comfort me. Sadly, because of the strained relationship with John, we were so distant that we couldn't be much comfort to each other.

Five-year-old Zach awoke the following day. "What's this thing in my arm?" he said.

"The IV. You are in the hospital."

He shouted, "What did you say?" We then discovered that he had sustained severe loss of hearing. He was a very sick little boy.

That evening, when my mom left the hospital for our home, she phoned. "Deanna, are you ready for more bad news? Your apartment has been robbed."

My precious treasures were stolen. Are you kidding? It wasn't expensive stuff, but it was mine. Another blow.

Twelve days and one operation later, a frail Zach was released from the hospital, weighing a mere thirty-five pounds. He was unable to walk and unable to hear, because the illness had killed the nerves that controlled both his balance and his hearing. We were thankful he was alive, and his tenacious spirit was so sweet.

Before Zach became ill, John had made plans to move into his own apartment. One week after Zach came home from the hospital, John was gone. I watched him move his stuff. We said our goodbyes. It was time for me to go back to my bedroom and cry.

A week later, I dropped off Zach at the preschool. He was frail, could hardly walk, and was afraid.

He cried.

I cried.

I had no choice. I was a single mom who had to work to pay the bills. Until you've had to do something like this, you can't imagine how heart-wrenching it was to leave him there. Of course, we adjusted.

I was broken-hearted on many levels, with three hurting boys— ages ten, seven, and five—who were looking to me for answers and comfort. My Texas family was so far away, they might as well have been in a foreign country. I spent many nights alone in my bedroom, on my mattress on the floor, crying. I was thirty-one years old and had never lived on my own before. Again, living alone had never been my dream. This was a nightmare.

44

Several months later, I moved back to Texas so I would have the support of family and friends. Being home felt wonderful, and the boys and I quickly adjusted to our new life. We lived with my parents, and I was grateful for their presence.

A couple years later, the boys and I moved to our own house in Denton. We were on our own now. I had a good job, and we loved our little house. The boys were growing—now fifteen, twelve, and ten. They struggled with their dad leaving, and Zach had trouble communicating and interacting with others. I had never dreamed of being a single mom, especially of all boys. Girls, I knew. Boys—they're different. My oldest son, Josh, was a teenager, taller than me, and full of attitude, not wanting to submit to a "girl." He challenged my authority. Since I had to work full-time to pay bills, the boys spent a lot of time at home alone, which was a concern to me. We were involved in a good church and seemed to be doing rather well.

Let's flash back a bit. I had known Jesus since I was six years old. We went to church as a family, and my parents lived the Christian life at home. While not perfect, it was a secure and loving childhood. Because of my early introduction to Jesus, I didn't have many outward problems or do a lot of bad things. I was not the rebellious one. I was studious, responsible, and a member of the National Honor Society. I was respectful of my parents and a good big sister (although there were those occasional knock-down, drag-outs with my next youngest sister—always her fault, of course).

So when I married young, I set out to prove I could have a happy marriage, be a stay-at-home mom, love the Lord, and raise good kids. As long as we could stay married and could go to church, I was proud of my life and how I was doing.

Unfortunately, this allowed me to feel I had the right to look down my nose at those who were not as "holy" as I was. I felt no remorse for judging others for *their* shortcomings and bad choices. I didn't recognize that I wasn't perfect either. When I found myself in the situation of having no husband and being a single parent, I understood what it felt like to be rejected and alone. I wasn't meant to be single. How was I ever going to meet my new Mr. Right? Where was my love?

What did I do in this situation? I made some of the same bad choices I had judged others for making. Doing the right thing wasn't always as easy as I had proclaimed. I fell hard off my righteous pedestal and landed on my face before God. In this way, God stripped away my self-proclaimed goodness and holiness. And He was not finished with me yet.

At 5:30 a.m. on July 29, 1993, the doorbell woke me up. Was I dreaming or had I imagined it? The doorbell rang again. I got up, threw on a robe, and peaked out to see an officer standing on my porch. When I opened the door, he asked if I remembered him from high school.

Was he driving around and just decided to stop and see me at this hour?

As we walked into the living room, he asked, "Are you living here alone with just the children?" When I answered yes, he said he had some bad news. Josh and three friends were in a car accident. Josh was killed. The three friends he was with received minor injuries. In a heartbeat, at fifteen years, seven months and twenty-one days young, Joshua Michael Kirkland was *gone*.

This is not a dream. This is real. This is not a dream. I have to call my parents before I lose it.

I remember my dad's voice as I woke him with the news and hearing my mom's exclamation of pain in the background. After that, I don't remember much.

People came in and out of my house. I wailed loudly as I sat on my bed, not caring who heard. Ten-year-old Zach tried to comfort me. When two pastors from our church showed up to talk with me, I said, "Doesn't God's Word say He will not give me more than I can handle? I think this might be too much."

It *was* too much for me, but it *wasn't* too much for God.

I decided to go to the funeral home with family for a private look at Josh. I signed in and turned around. An exclamation of shock escaped from me. There he was, lying in the casket. Wait. Something was very different. It was Josh. Then again, it was not. He was not there anymore. Just a shell of him lay there. His light, his personality, and mischievous grin were not there. My Josh was gone.

I don't do well at funerals. I get too emotional and identify with the bereaved too much. Now here I was, getting ready to attend my own son's funeral. How could I do this? I told my sister, "Sherry, I can't go. I can't do this." She gently got me into the car, and I went. A huge crowd was there with such an outpouring of support and love. I will never forget how God carried me and brought me through without my completely falling apart in tears.

Through the dark days that followed, I cried. I reminisced about Josh with friends and family, cried, tried to sleep, and then cried again. I also comforted my two younger boys, Caleb and Zach. We began a new adjustment period. After only one week, I went back to work. Many of those who saw me marveled that I was able to be there, surprised I could function properly after such a devastating event. The death of a child. It ranks up there in the category of "What could be worse?"

But God. Are there two more beautiful words in *any* language?

Just as I had found God to be faithful throughout my life, through a husband not loving me and divorce, through the devastating illness and ultimate disability of a child, and various other upheavals, I always found God to be a faithful Comforter—even through the death of my beloved son, Josh. I had heard His whispers of love to me throughout my life. I had felt alone, but I had never *really* been alone.

Living without Josh required many adjustments. I missed my big boy, his strength, and his help doing the "manly" stuff. I even missed his hairy teenage legs. My middle son, Caleb, struggled with guilt, because he knew Josh had gone out without telling me. Zach missed his big brother wrestling with him on the floor. We lost our only "man of the house." He was loved and remembered.

A couple months after Josh was gone, I was riding my bike through the neighborhood, talking to God. "Lord, I should not be able to function normally. Many tell me the grief will hit me hard years down the road, and *then* I will shut down. I should not be able to smile at this time. However, You are giving me strength. And if You want to carry me through in this way, it's okay with me." And that's what He did. God walked with me through those sad, lonely days through the tears, and at times, even giving laughter.

You can well imagine that at this point, I wondered if anything good would ever happen to me again. My normally optimistic outlook was severely dampened. Eight months later, I finally realized that my current hopeful romantic relationship was going nowhere, and I was again alone. I sat in my rocking chair in my bedroom and complained to God. "How am I ever going to meet anyone? I have two kids. I work full-time. No one will introduce me to anyone."

Boohoo.

If the truth were known, I was afraid that if I trusted God to send me a husband, He would send me someone so godly that I would drive the man crazy.

Then I heard God whisper in love to me again, as He assured me, *Deanna, I made you the way you are—with that crazy side and all. Why would I send a husband that wasn't perfect for you?* All I can say is that a weight lifted off my shoulders, and I finally trusted God with this part of my life.

A short time later, my mom told me of a conversation she and dad had with their best friends, Warren and Ina. While driving one day, Warren remarked to my parents that they prayed for me every day and felt God would send me a husband.

"You know who we need to introduce her to?" Warren said.

"Yes," Ina said. "Bill Martin."

They had known me since eighth grade and had known Bill about eight years. The timing had not yet been right for us to meet each other.

I got excited at hearing of this conversation. I thought, *This is a God thing.* Warren said he was going to give Bill a call and give him my number. So I waited, rather impatiently, I must confess. In a couple weeks, I got a call from Mom saying Bill lost my number and finally called Warren to get it.

Woohoo!

You can bet I was not going anywhere after work. I waited by the phone.

When Bill finally called, it went something like this:

Bill: "Hi, you don't know me, but we have a mutual friend."

I'm thinking, *I know, I've been waiting for you to call. What took you so long?*

Bill: "Would you like to go out for a sandwich on Thursday?"

A sandwich? "Who asks someone on a date for a sandwich?

We set the time for the coming week, and I couldn't wait. Thursday finally arrived, and I was getting ready for what could be my dream date when the doorbell rang. It was forty-five minutes before date time. It couldn't be him. But it was. I popped my head out of my bedroom and said I'd be just a minute. This was it.

We went to get the kids a "sandwich" (his name for burgers) and

48

immediately after ordering, he turned to me and asked, "What do you think went wrong with your first marriage?"

Seriously?

And the next three-and-a-half hours of this blind date were spent with him grilling me with questions on all aspects of life. Whew!

A short four weeks later, he proposed. Yes, he got down on one knee. Only four weeks more, and we tied the knot. He was indeed my *true* Prince Charming and made me feel like a princess.

That was twenty years ago. After so many devastating events, God brought me a wonderful husband. Yes, he is perfect for me. Of course, we have had our challenges, including marrying at an older age, trying to blend our two families, and having financial issues. Again and again, God has been so good, faithful to give us help through it all.

Now that you have heard *my* love story, I have a love story for *you*. I stand before you today letting you know that there is a God who loves you and wants to share Himself with you. Jesus came to save "sinners," people who are morally deficient. He wants to walk with you through your darkest minutes and give you times of joy, even amid the heartache.

If I had not personally known heartache, defeat, and disappointment, I could not relate to your pain and struggles. If I had continued in my pride and judgmental attitude, I could not look with compassion on your moral struggles. But God. He showed me myself and the darkness in my heart. He forgave me, and He can forgive you too.

Listen deep in your heart. Are you hearing His whispers of love to you? Do you long to have peace? To have joy, even though everything is not going the way you want? Consider Jesus. You may have heard of Him. If you have never trusted yourself to Him and asked Him to forgive you of your sins, you are lost. My son Joshua knew the Lord. He trusted Jesus, and I know he is in Heaven with God right now. I am confident I will see Him again one day. Josh did not know that July 29, 1993, would be his last day on Earth. Neither do you know when your time will be complete. Don't make the mistake of waiting until it is too late. Call out to Him right now.

Deanna Martin *was the oldest of four girls and married at nineteen. After thirteen years of marriage, she found herself entering the ranks of single, working moms. Over the years she experienced disability, divorce, and death. She met and married Bill. They owned and operated a vineyard for ten years. In the vineyard, God showed Deanna pictures of His love and care for His children. She wrote a book entitled,* Whispers in the Vineyard...A Vineyard Keeper's Meditations. *She currently writes a blog at* ***NannasGrapevine.blogspot.com.***

Thoughts to Ponder
from Whispers of Love

1. Human love is imperfect, but God's love is unfailing.

2. Prince Charming only exists in a fairy tale, but the Prince of Peace is reality.

3. When we need comfort, the Holy Spirit will whisper words of solace into our spirit.

What dreams do you need to give to God?

Come to me, all you who are weary and burdened, and I will give you rest. — Matthew 11:28

My Father's Great Sacrifice
by Rev. Dr. Penny Ruth W. Njoroge

In East Africa, school is not a given for girls. In fact, it's discouraged. Ever since I can remember, I always desired to go to school. For me to do so would take a great sacrifice by my father.

I am the first of ten children born to Lawrence and Miriam Macharia, a peasant family in Muranga, Kenya. My father was well-educated for his generation. My mother must have shared my desire to attend school, because her elder brother periodically sneaked her into class. This happened because my mother's mother died young, leaving the children predominantly under the care of their older brother, who also received some education and was determined to make a difference for his siblings. There, my mother learned to read and write—until her father found out and angrily stopped it.

I grew up when girls were raised to get married, have children, and take care of not only their own families but also the extended family. My paternal grandfather made it clear that none of his granddaughters would ever go to school. Like many men in his clan and generation, he strongly believed that educated girls were uncontrollable and would end up as prostitutes. I understood this, because giving daughters in marriage was a great family pride and was an investment due to the dowry that brought many cows, goats, and other gifts.

At age seven, I started caring for my siblings and other children that my mother adopted from the community. Their parents had died in our civil war. My mother had a heart for orphaned children, because she grew up as an orphan herself. She remembered the harsh treatment from her stepmother before her brother was old enough to support us. Because of my parents and with God's help, many of the children that we took in grew up and stood on their own.

When boys my age went to school, I was left behind to fetch firewood and water. I took care of our household needs, but I yearned to go with them to school. My father had to work, and my mother was busy growing food for the family. I didn't mind the responsibilities, but I resented being left out of school. The first

52

time I asked my parents about enrolling in classes, my father quickly reprimanded me. No girls in our family could go to school. He knew I loved my grandparents and the special place of honor I held as the oldest granddaughter. He warned me of the risk of losing this honor if I insisted on going to school.

My father's words didn't sway my deep desire for school or my growing resentment for not getting an education. I became withdrawn, sad, and restless. I hurried to finish my chores so I could sit by the boys and watch as they did their homework. Since I had no books, I copied what they were doing, writing on the dirt. No one thought this behavior was unusual, because they also practiced writing on dirt. Eventually, I tried to convince my mother. If given a chance to go to school, I was willing to wake up earlier and go to sleep late to ensure that all my household chores were done, the family water and firewood supply maintained.

Slowly, I gained my mother's sympathy by reminding her that I would make a better wife and mother if I could read my Bible and sing like she did from the Kikuyu hymn book. She often sang for us in the evenings or weekends when she was at home.

God answered my prayers in His own way and time. My mother talked to my father on my behalf, saying that perhaps they should enroll me in school. My father was apprehensive, since two daughters of a local chief had joined school, triggering negative comments and rumors. My parents kept my pleadings to themselves for the longest time. They constantly cautioned me on the serious consequences we would all face from my grandfather. However, I still couldn't give up my dream. I became increasingly angry with my grandparents, so much so that I wanted nothing to do with them anymore.

My grandfather asked why I had become so moody and quiet while serving them. Assuming my grandfather was getting genuinely concerned and would now understand, my father informed him that I was very persistent about going to school. He said I was getting depressed and hard to manage. My grandfather shouted at my father, loud enough for me to hear. None of his girls, especially me, would ever go to school. If my father made the mistake of enrolling me in school, he would be disowned, disinherited, and banished from his clan land.

I sat quietly behind our hut, not far from my grandparents' hut.

My father was quiet for what seemed like an eternity. In a very controlled voice, he respectfully explained to his father that he saw no reason to continue hurting his daughter, who was obedient and serving everyone in the household, including the grandparents, just because she desired an education. He pointed out that his wife, who happened to have received some education despite *her* father's disagreement, was the best wife he could ever want. He asked his father if there was anything that his daughter-in-law, who served the whole family effectively and intelligently, had ever done to annoy him. My grandfather loudly said he had nothing against my mother whose education he had no control over. However, his decision was final, and he had total control over what happened with his children and grandchildren. He would not tolerate any forced changes while he was living.

He then asked my father to summon my mother. My grandfather informed her of what he had just learned about my persistence for education. This plan was never to happen. Not only would he disown and disinherit my father and his family, but he would also put a curse on us. Nobody spoke about school after that, because the matter was getting out of hand. The placing of a curse on the family was the last thing anyone wanted.

My parents came home speechless. I was inside, pretending to warm myself at the fire with my siblings, a requirement when my parents weren't in the house. My mother led us in prayer about the future, asking for guidance. She then served dinner, and everyone ate quietly. I noticed that my parents barely ate. As soon as everyone finished, my siblings were sent to the bed we all shared. I was asked to remain behind to help clear the utensils, and I was updated on my father's conversation with his father, while my mother listened.

While I had already heard the entire conversation in hiding, I sat attentively and in shock. I wept as Dad explained the serious consequences facing our entire family if he enrolled me in school with my brothers. Tears welled up in my mother's eyes. As always, she reminded us that God was in control and would see us through everything.

I could not say anything at first. We were all quiet for a long while. Then I apologized for putting my parents into so much pain. I just didn't know how to kill that desire.

Having gone to school himself and having a slightly educated wife, my father appreciated my passion for education. He commended me for being helpful at home and being a good role model to my siblings and neighborhood kids. He said education would definitely be good for me. He thought I had potential in leadership and was very proud of me.

I sat speechless, not believing that my father would speak so positively about me after all the trouble I was causing.

My mother also said how proud she was of me. What a blessing I had been in helping raise my siblings and adopted cousins. They went on to say how well their friends and neighbors spoke of me, a daughter who was the envy of many families. With a light heart, trying to smile, my father talked about many of his friends who were already booking me as a future wife for their sons. The joke got out of hand when he said that an older man had offered him many cows to marry me as his fourth wife.

I jumped up and quickly told my father I hoped he had accepted nothing, because I would *never* marry an older married man.

They both asked me to calm down and listen to what they had decided.

My father believed that since my grandfather knew about my passion, conditions would only get worse for me. He would use me as a warning with serious consequences to ensure that none of his family members would ever consider girls' education again. Dad told me to continue serving them obediently as usual, but have very little conversation while he and my mother tried to figure out how to handle the situation.

I promised to do my best, as always, but pleaded with them to consider my own suffering. My mother hugged me and sent me to sleep.

The next few days were tense for us all. My grandmother, who loved talking and laughing with me, wanted to know why I was so quiet. I told her how busy I was, keeping up with my ever-increasing work. All my brothers were too consumed with schoolwork to help. Four weeks later, my father came home earlier than usual and asked us all to sit with him and mother and listen to their new plans.

I tensed, not sure what to expect.

He went straight to the point, informing us that we would be moving out of our rural home to Nairobi, where he had found a new job as a city bus conductor. My brothers would attend the school there. He made it even more beautiful, especially for me, when he promised that if I continued behaving well and helped my parents settle the family down in our new home, I would eventually be enrolled in school. He quietly and painfully explained as simply as possible that we would never inherit any ancestral land from his father. He and my mother had firmly decided that their daughters deserved education just like their brothers. The rest of the family did not agree with him, but we should hate no one for their lack of understanding. Instead, we should strive to become good role models, which might prepare a way for our girl cousins in the future. We were still very sad to leave our family and friends, but we were excited to move into the city.

While I was happy about joining a school, a new sense of sadness engulfed me when I realized that my father was abandoning his inheritance due to my insistence on going to school. While we were busy packing our few belongings, I tearfully promised to work hard all my life to ensure they never regretted their difficult decision.

They both hugged me, prayed over me, and assured me that their love and faith in me was greater than I would ever know. They were confident God would give them much more in life than what they were leaving behind. They asked me to promise I would make every effort to continue loving, respecting, and honoring my grandparents, praying that God would one day help them understand why I wanted education so badly.

My family relocated, but joining school took much longer than I had anticipated. An emergency was declared in my country when my people rebelled against the British colonial masters, demanding self-governance and eventual independence. Like many men and women, my father was detained several times. My mother started growing food for the family along the Nairobi river, irrigating with sewer water. She sold some of the vegetables at the farmer's market to sustain and educate our family. While working in a hospital, I always washed my hands and used hand sanitizer. Mother prayed that we would never become sick from the sewer water we walked in and touched, the same water that irrigated the vegetables that we ate and sold. The memory of that causes me to fully trust in God's protection.

At age eleven, I started school, joining children much younger than me. Constantly aware of what it had cost my father and family, I lived with the passion and pressure to excel. My parents would never regret educating me against their family traditions. While helping my mother with household chores and raising my siblings, I worked very hard in class. At times, I advanced two classes in a year, which let me catch up with my peers. With my mother's constant reminder that I was a trailblazer, opening education for other girls, I became a very high achiever, often maintaining first position in class.

When I was fourteen, my grandparents visited us in Nairobi a few weeks before schools closed for the Christmas holidays. This appeared good and necessary, since my parents had tried to maintain friendly communication with them. I gladly served and entertained them.

They stayed with us for a week. They sat with my parents for hours in the evening, but the children were forced to go to sleep early to give them space. Barely a week after school closed, my cousin came to visit. A day later, a few aunties also came to visit, which got me a bit suspicious. The next day, early Friday morning around three o'clock, my cousin and I were rudely awakened by several women who were singing and dancing.

Without warning, they hurried us into the shower and undressed us. I instantly knew what to expect when each of us were pinned down by two strong women and put through traditional circumcision, now widely known as FGM (Female Genital Mutilation). It happened so fast, the excruciating pain and the accompanying bleeding was beyond words for either of us. We knew it was still being practiced in our culture, but we had hoped that living in the city might have saved us from facing it all.

Today, as I relive the experience, my body goes into emotional and physical spasms. At times, I still feel anger at finding out that this was the reason my grandparents had visited. They came to warn my parents that putting me into school caused the clan to insist on undergoing FGM or be openly cursed by my grandparents. I questioned my parents about why the circumcision had to happen, but they quickly explained that they feared any further consequences from disobeying their parents.

Their response put me on a warpath. I boldly challenged my parents to prove this procedure's biblical relevance. It was a daily discussion. I swore that while I lived, none of my younger sisters would ever experience that pain. If my mother's women friends visited and spent the night at our home, I never slept. I made it clear to my mother that I would scream to everyone if they ever attempted FGM on my sisters.

Eventually, my mother agreed it was a cruel and totally unnecessary tradition that did more damage than good. Some girls bled to death or got an infection. I thank God for His intervention. None of my sisters were circumcised. Even though it is, unfortunately, still practiced in some tribes, I thank God that my daughters, granddaughters, and numerous other girls in their generations will never experience this. It reminds me of my mother's words that I would be a trailblazer in many things. I became the sacrificial lamb to break the curse, building my resilience, empowering me to fight, protecting others.

In 1963, I successfully completed primary school at Kenya Certificate of Primary Education as the second-best girl student in Kenya's capital city of Nairobi. This automatically earned me a place in Alliance Girls High School in Kikuyu, the best high school for gifted girl students. This was a great honor for me and my family after all we had gone through, struggling with school fees, missing school often, and going hungry. My parents sometimes couldn't provide even the basic needs like clothes and books. It was tough, but despite the poverty, God prevailed in paving a way for education for all my siblings. My parents were overjoyed and grateful. They kept reminding us that eventually God would repay them for everything they had lost by sacrificially choosing to educate their daughters.

In December 1967, I joined the National Christian Council of Kenya as a trainee secretary, going to college in the mornings and working afternoons and some Saturdays. While still supporting my family, I married Isaac in 1969, my high school friend. We had three sons and a daughter. The marriage lasted thirty years, but the physical abuse was so bad that I attempted suicide twice. The abuse happened at a time when the African woman was only to be seen and rarely heard. There was also economic, emotional, physical, and psychological abuse supported by the culture and traditions where

58

the man had total control over his wife. The only thing that kept me in my marriage was wanting my kids to grow up in a family. I believed in faith that God would heal it. I desired to advance myself to earn a better living for my immediate family and continued helping my other family members.

Eventually, the abuse became too much for me and my children, who were also deeply affected by watching my great suffering. While my husband provided materially and took the children to good schools to protect his public image, I suffered from hidden depression. I became suicidal after realizing what it had done to my children, especially my daughter and youngest son. However, I survived and ended up in the hospital for a month. There, I decided to take a leap of faith and venture into a new horizon of my life. Regardless of the societal expectations and consequences I might face, I would leave my marriage when I left the hospital.

I took the risk of renting an apartment in a gated boarding school, where my children and I lived for a year before finding our way to the United States in 2000. I literally ran for my life, deeply yearning for a new beginning for me and my children. Like Abraham, I fled my country, not sure what awaited me in the United States. All I brought with me were two suitcases, a Bible, our passports, and my high school diploma.

The next couple of years were scary. It was difficult to process a painful long-distance divorce, but I was ready to survive or die. Faith and total dependence on God became the wind that carried me through several harrowing experiences with no money or family to help us. For once in my life, I knew God alone would rescue us. I arrived in Birmingham, Alabama, on a J1 visa to train as a hospital chaplain. I recognized I would never realize my dream of becoming a cardiologist.

I enrolled my youngest son in a community college for his computer engineering degree. I trained at Carraway hospital for a small stipend during the day and sat with patients in nursing homes at night to feed and house my family and pay tuition for my son. He could not qualify for scholarships, because he was an international student. My daughter cleaned houses and offices. All along, I still dreamed of college so I could get a better job. I wanted to support my children as a single mother and still support my parents who were elderly and in poor health. My chaplain position required my ordination and a Master's Degree in Theology or Divinity. However, all I brought to the States was my high school diploma.

Through it all, God fulfilled the deep desire I had to bring my parents to the United States for a visit so they could reconnect with their grandchildren. The Anglican church I attended planned to ordain me in April 2001, but my husband and I were not formally divorced. So he blocked the ordination through the Archbishop of Kenya and the Bishop of Alabama. Later that year, we were divorced. My parents visited in 2002, and that was the last time I saw my father alive.

They blessed each of us in a formal ceremony in my house and thanked me for keeping my promise of never disappointing them after all they had lost. They felt God had rewarded them tremendously, not only because of what I had achieved but also because it had opened opportunities for other girls in the community. This included some nieces and children of the brothers and clansmen who had disowned and disinherited them for educating me.

Upon my son's graduation with his bachelor's degree, at age fifty-six I enrolled myself for distant learning with Carolina University of Theology. I finished my Certified Professional Education (CPE) training and started training as a CPE Supervisor. Six months into my Bachelor's Degree in Theology and a new mortgage, Carraway hospital closed the Pastoral Care Department, forcing me to look for another job.

In June 2003, I joined St. Vincent's East Ascension Hospital as a Certified Nursing Assistant and eventually worked as a hospice chaplain for four years before becoming a hospital chaplain. As a trauma chaplain, I worked in different units like labor and delivery, critical care units, and the ER. I pursued education passionately, graduating in 2009 with honors with a Ph.D in Christian Counseling Psychology. I majored in mental illness, alcohol and substance abuse, and grief therapy. I was board-certified as a Clinical Psychiatric Chaplain, as a Substance Abuse Therapist, as a Death and Grief Therapist, and as a Marriage and Family Therapist.

I was selected to lead spirituality support groups and individual counseling in our eighty-bed Behavioral Health Center, serving clients from nineteen to ninety years. I am a passionate advocate for the mentally ill, as well as those battling different addictions to drugs and alcohol. By God's doing and grace alone, I became an award-winning transformational speaker against FGM, domestic violence, and discrimination against women and children. My work and interaction with people in these situations humbles me and reminds me that were it not for God's grace, I should be the one in these centers. He has also carried my children through the storms and is using them too.

I have traveled many miles encouraging people not to look down on anyone. No one knows God's plans, not even the poorest and simplest among us. It took forty-one years from high school to receiving my Ph.D at age sixty-two.

Raised in the poorest Nairobi slums, barely surviving, I am thankful for all that God has done. He is using my life story to encourage others. I received awards from the President of Kenya for community service in Kenya. In the United States, I received the Alabama Hospital Heroes award, the Birmingham Mayor's Hidden Heroes award for Youth Mentoring, and the 2015 International Most Motivating Woman of the Year award. I am also a Fellow of the American Institute of Stress.

Glory to God for all He has done for me and my children. May this story motivate and uplift others to fight for their dreams, allowing God to turn their scars into stars bright enough to light people's paths. Some things are worth the sacrifice.

Rev. Dr. Penny Ruth W. Njoroge has been a Counseling Psychologist, psychotherapist, and group therapist for over 25 years. She is a Board-Certified therapist in substance abuse and addictions, death and grief, marriage and family, as well as crisis intervention. She is a Fellow of American Institute of Stress and a Diplomate with American Academy of Experts in Traumatic Stress/National Center for Crisis Management. She has received the Birmingham Caregiver of the Year award, Alabama Hospital Hero's award, and Kenya's Presidential award for Community Service. Rev. Dr. Njoroge tweets from @DrPennyOnline.

Thoughts to Ponder
from My Father's Great Sacrifice

1. If a desire is God-given, He will help you realize it.

2. God doesn't take your sacrifices lightly.

3. God faithfully provides for those who trust Him.

Are you persistently following God's call, whatever the cost?

Let us not become weary in doing good, for at the proper time we will reap a harvest if we do not give up. — Galatians 6:9

A Shining Light
by Gale Duran

"Let your light shine before others, that they may see your good deeds and glorify your Father in heaven" (Matthew 5:16).

Matthew 5:16 has always been my life verse. I was given that verse by my dear dad when I was a little girl. Why did he give me that verse? I am glad you asked.

We were carving a pumpkin for Halloween, and my dad put the candle in the pumpkin. When I saw the light shining, I said, "Punky." I was trying to say *pumpkin*, but from that moment on, my nickname was Punky. That is when my dad told me I should always let my little light shine.

I was raised by my mother and father on a dairy farm in northwest Ohio. I had two sisters and a big brother. We made it a family tradition to work together doing the farm chores—milking the cows, feeding the calves, and helping with the baby pigs. Our family was together 24/7, everyone pitching in.

Every weekend, we attended Sunday school and church. It was a day of worship and rest.

My grandparents were also an important part of my family of origin.

As time went on, I attended a summer church camp, and that is where I made a serious confession to accept Christ as my Lord and Savior. I understood how Jesus came to die for my sins so I could be forgiven. I also knew He loved me unconditionally. The Bible told me I was a sinner, and all sin keeps us from having a personal relationship with Christ. God's Word also said the wages of sin is death, but the gift of God is eternal life. When we ask forgiveness of those wrong things in our lives, we are forgiven. I wanted to know Jesus with my whole heart and soul. I wanted to be forgiven for any wrong I'd done.

My little light shined all over the neighborhood. I understood that I was created in the image of God, and I was loved by Him. He desired a relationship with me, and that changed my life. No longer did I need the approval of those around me. I had a desire to know more about Jesus Christ and His plan for my life.

As I grew older, my dad bought me a horse. One day when he

went to the barn to care for my horse, he stepped on a rusty nail. This placed him in the hospital with a serious bone infection. My dad recovered, but this is where my testimony gets exciting. My dad's hospital roommate was a handsome man who became a very good friend. He asked me to marry him, and we had an amazing life together. We brought two beautiful daughters into the marriage and had a great little family. We hosted family picnics and attended county fairs and parades. We went to family reunions together, and yes, we planned many vacations.

However, over the years my husband drank more and more excessively, until his drinking became a problem in our marriage. By the time the drinking got really bad, our daughters were adults in college. Time had flown past so quickly that the change in my husband seemed like it had happened overnight, even though it was a gradual progression. My husband started to hide liquor in his truck to keep me from seeing the extent of his alcohol consumption. It was then, after twenty-three years of marriage, that I received a phone call that forever changed my life. The voice on the phone asked me to come to the local hospital. When I arrived, I was told that my forty-four-year-old husband was dead on arrival after a massive heart attack.

What now, God? What do I do? Where do I go? What can I do all alone?

This is when I learned that even when your husband dies, God is always with you. In the Bible, He promises never to leave nor forsake us. Never! I fell on my knees and cried out to God: "Give me direction and ideas of what to do now, please." I continued to beg God for a reply.

The answer came in an open door. I was called by Southwest Texas State University to teach during the day and earn my graduate degree at night. This was unbelievable—I thought my world was falling apart and suddenly, it was falling into place.

Was I in shock? Yes.

Was I overwhelmed? Yes.

Was I scared half to death? Yes.

Was God asking me to leave my family and friends in Ohio to move to Texas? I wanted to trust and obey—but leave Ohio—really? I searched the Bible for answers, and the verse I found said to lean on God with your whole heart and not to lean on your own understanding. So I took that as a sign and moved to Texas. I started teaching and worked on my Master's Degree at the same time.

It was amazing that my move to Texas was at the same time my parents sold the family farm and relocated to McAllen, Texas, to retire. Wow, God—who would have ever guessed my family would also become Texans?

However, I was still grieving over the loss of my husband and the transition of moving to Texas. One day, as I was in the clubhouse at my new apartment complex, I broke down and sobbed violently. The manager of the apartments asked me what was wrong. I told her what had happened, and guess what. Even though she was a stranger to me, she laid her hands on my shoulders and prayed for me. What an amazing blessing from God. I will never forget her act of kindness that brought so much peace and courage to me.

I met a lot of new friends. Many put their arms around me and lifted my spirits. They encouraged me and helped my faith to grow. I went to a local church's singles group and met new friends who shared many struggles similar to mine. The Bible studies were powerful, and many of the singles had lost their spouses in car accidents, from cancer, and from other calamities.

The president of the group started to show me attention, and he asked me out on a date. I soon learned that he really loved his Lord and Savior, had never been married, and did not want to have children. Was God showing up in my empty life with blessings or what? This single man worked in a local hospital, and I was finishing my graduate degree. Once my degree was completed, I landed an amazing job. As time went on, we saw each other more and more.

One evening, we were sitting on the banks of the San Marcos River. He popped the question and asked me to marry him. Yes, I was confused, shocked, and happy, all at the same moment. I had told God I did not want to date or marry again, but if it was His will, then the man had to love God, not want children, never have been married before, and oh yes, it would be wonderful if he lived on a farm. I am sure you have already figured out that God put this man in my life with all those qualities and most importantly, he loved me.

Amazing!

God had his fingerprints all over my new life and had placed the man of the puzzle pieces into my lap. Now the girls would have an amazing stepdad, and the grandkids would have a loving grandpa.

I searched the Bible and found Jeremiah 29:11. "For I know the plans I have for you," declares the Lord, "plans to prosper you and not to harm you, plans to give you hope and a future."

God had a purpose and plan for me, and it was to be good and prosperous. That's just like our God, right? Now, I saw why God had moved me to Texas to start my life over. I never, in my wildest dreams, thought I would meet another man and get married again. However, I placed my life in God's hands and trusted and obeyed His will for my life, with amazing results.

Over time, our lives were filled with God and His unconditional love. Our lives are not perfect, but we study the Bible, follow His leading, and increase our faith in His will every day. Today, my husband and I both lead Bible study groups and mentor younger Christians in the faith walk. For a time, we worked for the "Family Life" ministry in Arkansas. That was a true blessing. Now, we are both retired and continue to be new creations in Christ. We pray out loud together and keep Christ at the center of our marriage, knowing that Satan wants to destroy marriages and families. We also serve Him in jail ministries and in our local church.

We urge everyone to follow the Ten Commandments, and His blueprints for their lives. We must let our lights shine all over the place. God is good, and He is good *all* the time. Our lives have changed, our spirits are bright, and we hope our lives are a blessing to others.

Like my life, many times we do not understand or agree with what happens, but remember, God has a plan and a very special purpose for each of us.

We are all sons and daughters of the King of kings and Lord of lords. So let your light shine before men, and when they see your good works, they will give glory to God. Amen and amen!

Gale Duran *teaches and writes about adoption in hopes of encouraging other families to care for the millions of unwanted children in the world. She holds a Master's Degree in Communication from Texas State University. She resides in Texas with her husband, two daughters, and four grandchildren.* *GaleDuran.com*

Thoughts to Ponder
from A Shining Light

1. God calls us all to shine His light.

2. When we experience heartbreak, the Lord has a plan to restore us.

3. God's Word provides clear direction.

How can you shine God's light during the good and the bad?

You are the light of the world. A town built on a hill cannot be hidden. — Matthew 5:14

Leaving Intentional Fingerprints
by Wanda Strange

The administrator of the clinic stood before a group of my colleagues and friends and said, "Wanda, you have made a difference in so many people's lives—too many to count. You have had the honor of doing what you love, and it shows. You have spread happiness, hope, and knowledge. You give of yourself and share your words. Thank you for all your contributions. You made a difference every single day. You leave your work life to move onto your next adventure, where you will continue to make a difference."

As she completed her remarks, she placed a canvas in my hands. "This heart was made with the fingerprints of your colleagues, physicians, and most importantly, patients and family members. Let it remind you of the significant difference you have made."

As a little girl at church camp, I listened to the missionaries share stories of their work and of the needs around the world. My tender heart responded, and I began my journey of listening for God's voice. Perhaps I would be a missionary nurse. It sounded exciting and fulfilling. By the time I entered junior high school, I realized God's path for me did not include serving on the mission field. However, the pull to a career in nursing remained strong.

A slight detour sidetracked my route to a nursing career. Fourteen days after graduation, I married my high school sweetheart, so I took a clerical job in a physician's office. For a time, I silenced the voice in my spirit and settled for a paycheck instead of a purpose.

Though I accepted Christ as a small child, I possessed an immature faith, drifted spiritually, and relegated God to a small corner of my life. If I listened for God's voice at all, I pushed it to the back of my mind. I found myself stuck in a rut. Unsatisfied. Unfulfilled. Unhappy. I yearned for something more.

As I sought a deepening relationship with God, the desire to pursue nursing education grew stronger. I surrendered to God's calling for my life, returned to school, and worked in nursing for over four decades. I never considered oncology nursing as an option. How could I possibly remain detached enough to make a difference? I imagined myself in a puddle of tears beside the patient, unable to function or be of assistance to anyone. However, God had a better plan. I spent the last fifteen years of my career caring for cancer patients and their family members. My colleagues and I agree—oncology nursing is both the most difficult and most rewarding job you will ever love.

In 2010, I accepted a position as an oncology nurse navigator. The administration hired me, despite my lesser level of education than what was required by the job description. My experience and temperament made me the perfect fit for the job. My work consisted of assisting patients as they navigated the cancer treatment journey. I experienced fulfillment as I bonded with individuals and supported them physically, emotionally, and spiritually.

Throughout my nursing career, I gave 100 percent. After six years in the navigator role, I eagerly anticipated the life I had planned for retirement. Emotionally and physically exhausted, my first order of business in retirement was rest, and rest I did. For the first few weeks, I seldom left my house. Then I attacked the house—cleaning with a vengeance and catching up on much-neglected projects.

Before boredom set in, I made plans to engage in church and community activities. My calendar filled up, and I found myself quite busy. I considered the retirement possibilities. Volunteer options abounded. I filled the time with book club, garden club, Bible studies, line dance, water aerobics, reading, writing, travel—all the things I had neglected while pursuing a career. So much to do—so little time—yet a void simmered in my spirit.

Much of my personal identity and fulfillment resulted from caring for the needs of patients and caregivers. I loved nursing in general and oncology nursing in particular. What a blessing. I spent my days in a fulfilling profession. God placed me in that position, and I understood my purpose.

Those character traits and spiritual gifts that allowed me to minister throughout my career still resided in me. As I determined how to spend my days, I considered which activities fulfilled my calling.

On my retirement day, I relinquished my work identity. However, I didn't turn in my brain with my office keys. I didn't surrender my nursing knowledge or lose my compassion. Instead, I gained the freedom to choose how to spend my days. No longer tied to a rigid schedule, I explored new opportunities and renewed my commitment to my life's purpose.

What activities best utilize my knowledge and gifts?

How do I best honor God?

Where is He leading me?

God designed us for fellowship with Him and created us for a purpose. We only find fulfillment when we live in harmony with His purpose for our lives. Recognizing my yearning for fulfillment, I reordered my priorities.

- Time alone with God—Bible study—Prayer—Reflection
- Care of my own physical needs and for my family
- Worship
- Develop a strategy to identify and reach those who need support
- Encourage others through visits, phone calls, and written words
- Relaxation and renewal

As I honor the commitment, my joy and contentment resurge. I sense His presence more fully, and I feel His pleasure.

Three of my role models fully illustrate living God's purpose throughout life. They continue to inspire me to actively pursue my calling.

First is the unofficial ambassador of our small town, who moved into an assisted living facility under duress. His health deteriorated and left him unable to live alone in his home. He worried about who would fulfill his role, welcoming newcomers in the community. Throughout his retirement years, he visited every new resident to the small town and invited them to church. He made certain they experienced a warm welcome. Settling into his new home, he found a new ministry. Instead of visiting the new residents of his small town, he visits the residents of the assisted living facility and brings a welcome smile to lonely seniors. Though his location has changed, his purpose remains the same. He is ninety-one.

Second is our church pianist retired from teaching elementary school. She continues to play the piano every Sunday, exercises regularly, plays forty-two and chicken foot weekly, organizes benevolence meals, bakes the best chocolate chip cookies for every event, hosts a sewing circle, book club, regular ladies' gatherings, and faithfully participates in the intercessory prayer group. Her age is eighty-eight.

Third is Grandmommy Cargile, my grandmother-in-law, who died over forty years ago. She was over eighty. While in the nursing home, she participated in ceramics, painted, and led Bible studies for the residents. As her health declined, she continued to encourage her children and grandchildren by praying for them and writing letters and cards of encouragement. Those written communications still serve to inspire her family members.

I retired at age sixty-five. If God allows me to live as long as my role models, I desire to spend the decades ahead making a difference in the lives of others.

The treasured retirement gift, a colorful canvas, occupies a prominent area in my home, where it continues to remind me of my purpose. The multicolored heart represents the many people who intentionally left fingerprints on my heart. The rays of color emanating from the heart prompt me to seek ways to reflect God's love and compassion. As long as I breathe, He gives me opportunities to fulfill His purpose.

Wanda Strange and her husband, Kerry, native Texans, reside in Bluff Dale. Her active life prioritizes faith, family, and friends. An active member of her church and community, she devotes time to reading, writing, music, and volunteering. Though retired since 2016, love of oncology nursing inspires her to encourage patients, caregivers, and colleagues. Her passion for people provides motivation to share stories of God's faithfulness. August 2018, she released Emerging from the Crucible: Enduring God's Refining Fire.

WStrange0306@gmail.com
Facebook.com/WandaDoolyStrange

Thoughts to Ponder
from Leaving Intentional Fingerprints

1. God created us for a purpose.

2. The most fulfilling life results when we live in harmony with God's purpose.

3. We may retire from the daily work force, but we never retire from the purpose to which God calls us.

> **No matter your age, how can you be intentional in fulfilling your purpose?**

For we are God's handiwork, created in Christ Jesus to do good works, which God prepared in advance for us to do. — Ephesians 2:10

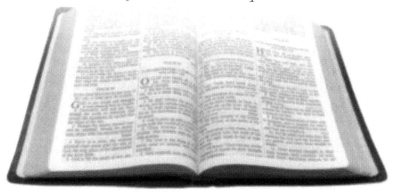

Secrets
by Susan Lewis

Have you ever had a secret? A secret you didn't want anyone to know?

I'm going to share some of my secrets with you.

I'm a Dallas girl, born and raised, but how I got to Big D is kind of funny. My mom was a nurse sent from Chicago to Dallas for work in the late 1940s. My dad was a New-Englander with roots dating back to the Mayflower. He was stationed in Texas for training during World War II. While in Texas, he dated and decided he really liked Texas women. After the war, he returned to find himself a Texas woman but instead met and married my mom from Chicago. He joked that he didn't marry a Texas woman, but he raised one.

I grew up in a loving home. Looking back, I realize that our family didn't talk about our feelings. We put a smile on every situation. At an early age, I learned to stuff my feelings. I was the "perfect child," always doing the right thing, but my older brother was always getting into trouble.

Did you have a "time out" chair" in your home? We had a small house with a special chair in the corner of the living room. When one of us did something wrong, Mom sat us in the "time out chair." One day when I was three years old, I put myself in the "time out" chair and turned to face the corner. Mom never knew what I did wrong, but I apparently thought I needed to be punished. I said, "Mommy, nobuddy's puwfect."

I wanted to be perfect. Guess what. I wasn't perfect. However, at Sky Ranch Camp when I was nine, I learned about someone who was—Jesus. The college-age counselors were loving others in a way I'd never seen before, and I was drawn to that love. Our counselor said, "Anyone who isn't sure they are going to Heaven, come talk to me." I was too embarrassed to say anything, so my girlfriend spoke up for me. Our counselor explained that if we asked Jesus to be our Savior, He would walk through this life with us. He paid for everything we had done or would do that was wrong, and He prepared a place for us in Heaven. From that moment, I knew Jesus was with me, and I committed my life to follow Him. I learned the importance of reading the Bible, because that's God's instruction manual for our lives.

When I was eleven, a tumor appeared on the back of my head, and I had surgery. But the tumor grew back. The second time, more-extensive surgery was needed, so my head was mostly shaved. No one thought to warn me that my head would be shaved. They just wheeled me on the gurney into a small room, and a Frenchman shaved off my hair. I was shocked and embarrassed, but dutifully swallowed my feelings and went through the surgery.

Remember, I was thirteen.

For six months, I wore a wig, desperately hoping no one would notice. Embarrassed, I didn't want anyone to discover my secret. A month after the surgery, I lined up with all the other campers in front of the trading post, waiting to go to the campfire. I was wearing my girlfriend's sailor cap, and she jokingly said, "I want my hat." She snatched it right off my head. Unfortunately, there on the ground in front of us was not only her cap but also my wig. I looked for a hole in the ground where I could disappear. I grabbed my hair and ran back to the cabin, totally humiliated.

That year, I started a new junior high school where I didn't know many people. One of the popular girls met me in the hall, with her handsome boyfriend on her arm. "Is that a wig you're wearing?" she said. I have no idea how I responded, but they obviously knew my secret. Once again, I wanted to find a hole and hide.

Despite these embarrassing events in my teenage years, many wonderful things happened. I was elected cheerleader in both junior high and high school, which forced me out of my shyness. I was Senior Class Favorite, an A student, and a committed Christian. I even helped lead a weekly Bible study at school. Outwardly, I appeared to be happy and well-adjusted, the "perfect student," but no one knew my secrets. I was living in shame, addiction, and self-hatred, a precursor to years of depression.

When I was thirteen, my best friend from another school said, "Susan, I learned this neat trick. We can eat whatever we want, and then just throw up." This was thrilling news. I didn't have to worry about gaining weight. I had always seen myself as fat, even as a young child. With all my dieting, I had never been able to lose the five or ten pounds I thought I needed to lose. What I didn't realize was that this "trick" was actually a trap, leading to a food addiction and related issues.

When I was growing up, we didn't know about "eating disorders." In the early 1980s, I first read about "bulimia" and "anorexia" in a magazine. I was shocked. I thought, *Oh my gosh! I'm not the only freak.* I felt like a Dr. Jekyl and Mr. Hyde, appearing as one person on the outside but struggling intensely when I was alone. I was behaving badly by not taking care of my body, which the Bible calls the temple of the Holy Spirit, but I was addicted. I continued to stuff my feelings with food. With my identity tied to my body size, I never felt thin enough.

My identity was also tied to my hair. After my head was shaved at age thirteen, I subconsciously made a vow to always have long hair. For many years, my hair fell below my waist. These were my secret idols: thinness and long hair—along with people-pleasing and perfectionism. My idols and the lies I told myself became the chains for my bondage. I was just like the Israelites in the wilderness, only no one could see my golden calves.

In author Beth Moore's *Breaking Free* study, she says, "Jesus came to set the captive free, but Satan came to make the free captive." I was committed to following Jesus. I was supposed to be living in freedom, yet I was held captive by the lies I believed. Satan was accomplishing his goals. He wants God's people trapped and living in bondage. Beth Moore also says, "The seeds to a stronghold are often planted with a lie."

Some of the lies I had chosen to believe were:

- I needed to be perfect.
- I was never thin enough.
- My hair was never long enough or pretty enough.
- I needed to please everyone.

I had secret strongholds in my life—things that kept me trapped.

In my freshman year of college, my dates with Rick were getting serious. I thought, *I must tell him my secrets.* His response showed his heart of love toward me, and I think some very deep insight. "I can't believe you punish yourself like that," he said.

I had never seen myself that way, as if I were the little three-year-old Susan who punished herself by sitting in the corner for not being perfect.

The Minirith Clinic, a counseling center, states, "Shame is the root of all addictions. It may be forgotten, hidden, or disguised, but the shame is there, it is real, and it drives behavior." In her study, Beth Moore says, "Shame is Satan's stamp of approval." God knows that shame is a real struggle. The Bible says God will take away the shame of our youth (Hebrews 12:2). Jesus endured the cross and scorned the shame.

I thought, *Surely I won't still be struggling with food-issues after I get married.* But I was wrong. There were days as a newlywed that I asked Rick to put a chain and padlock on our refrigerator, because I couldn't trust myself to have any self-control.

Next, I thought, *Surely I won't still be struggling when I'm pregnant.* Again, I was wrong. I ate such small amounts of food during my first pregnancy that a month before my due date, my placenta started leaking. I was confined to bed for the last two weeks before the baby came, but I was proud of the fact that I had gained only ten pounds. I was a college-educated young adult, but I was blinded to the truth. I thought I was being healthy. The bulimic or anorexic mind doesn't always see reality.

I don't know what would have become of me if I hadn't had God's Word to cling to. After putting my little boys down for their naps, I found comfort in the Psalms, where the writers cried out to the Lord. They had words when I had none. As in Psalm 77, some of them struggled like me.

When I was twenty-nine, a friend came for a pastor's conference and stayed with us. He was one who prayed for the sick and afflicted, and for those in bondage. When I began to tell my secrets, he said, "Susan, that's why the Lord brought me to Dallas—to pray for you."

As we prayed, the Holy Spirit revealed more secrets that I needed to confess. Our friend prayed that strongholds would be broken and that any evil influences would leave. Nothing dramatic happened, but we believed God had begun a good work in me. In a dream that night, a girlfriend came to my house and gave me a new dress—red and green, the colors of Christmas. I put it on, and when I woke up, I felt that God had clothed me in new garments of praise.

I wish I could say I was suddenly and completely set free. Instead, that day marked a turning point. Psalm 40:2 says, "He lifted me out of the slimy pit, out of the mud and mire; he set my feet on a rock and gave me a firm place to stand." I prayed this scripture many times. "Lord," I said, "thank You for bringing me out of the pit of destruction. Please give me a firm place to stand. Teach me how to relate to food, to myself, and to others."

Our prayer time with our pastor friend was just the first of many significant steps in the recovery process. I received help from professional counselors as well.

When I was thirty-one and pregnant with our third son, I recognized my need to deal with unforgiveness. My pastor's wife prayed with me, and we invited the Holy Spirit to be our divine Counselor. She sensed many issues in my life that pointed back to when I was thirteen. As we prayed, I remembered having my head shaved, and for the first time, I cried about that loss. For almost twenty years, I had stuffed those feelings, but now an emotional dam burst and I sobbed and sobbed. I felt the healing comfort of the Lord and knew He had been with me during the surgery.

We dealt with many issues as we continued to pray. My friend said, "Susan, I think you're supposed to cut your hair, which still fell below my waist. I had been sensing the same thing. Tearing down that idol in my life brought more freedom. Another weight was lifted off my shoulders.

Undoing the enemy's lies can be a slow process. My healing came through the following:

1. **Prayer and confession.** James 5:16 says, "Therefore confess your sins to each other and pray for each other so that you may be healed. The prayer of a righteous person is powerful and effective." It takes both our prayers and the prayers of our brothers and sisters.

2. **Receiving the unconditional forgiveness of Jesus.** His death on the cross was enough to pay for all my sins and unfaithfulness to Him. In addition to His forgiveness, we must allow Him to heal our wounds. Whether our bondages came through our own sins or something done to us doesn't matter. God can bring healing and freedom.

3. **Accepting the love of the Father.** Brennan Manning says in his book *Ruthless Trust*, "Our trust in Jesus grows as we shift from making self-conscious efforts to be good to

allowing ourselves to be loved as we are (not as we should be)."

4. **Outside counsel.** I received help from counselors, which is often very beneficial.

5. **The Holy Spirit.** Ezekiel 36:26 says, "I will give you a new heart and put a new spirit in you; I will remove from you your heart of stone and give you a heart of flesh." Many times I have prayed for Him to remove the stony places in my heart and to give me a heart of flesh.

6. **The Word of God.** Ecclesiastes 12:1 says, "Remember your Creator in the days of your youth, before the days of trouble come." We all have troubles in our lives, and if we turn to our Creator, He will redeem us and draw near to us.

As I was being healed of eating disorders, the Lord gave me the gift of dance. Since 1992, a small dance ministry has been a huge blessing in my life. Isaiah 61:3 says God will "provide for those who grieve in Zion—to bestow on them a crown of beauty instead of ashes, the oil of joy instead of mourning, and a garment of praise instead of a spirit of despair." This scripture reminds me of my dream when I was given a new dress.

He has brought beauty out of my life.

Sometimes people think, if you're a Jesus-follower, life will be easy. The Bible doesn't say that. Jesus said, "In this world you will have trouble. But take heart! I have overcome the world" (John 16:33).

In life, we must be prepared to experience the good and the bad. A friend unexpectedly called me in April of 2006 to share Isaiah 45:3. It said that God will give you treasures of darkness and riches stored in secret places, that you may know He is the Lord, and has called you by name. I thought, *Oh great, this doesn't sound very good. Treasures of Darkness?*

Those dark days came. I was the primary caregiver for all four parents as well as an aunt in Massachusetts. We dealt with cancer, Alzheimer's, strokes, and heart attacks.

My favorite prayer became, "Thank you, Father."

During our difficulties, there were many gifts. We were given a trip with friends to Cuernevaca. We also had weddings. Can you believe all three of our daughters-in-law invited me to shop with them and their moms for their wedding dresses? Me, the mother of three boys!

During this period, I believe I audibly heard God's voice. I was awakened one morning when I heard my name called. "Susan." I jumped out of bed and heard *That you may know I am the Lord, and have called you by name* (Isaiah 45:3).

I was exhausted beyond anything I could remember. I worked many twelve- to fifteen-hour days, and Rick ended up with bronchitis three times. Rick's mother died on Valentine's Day.

In May, barely able to put one foot in front of the other, I flew to Chicago for a buying trip. Rick stayed home, recovering from his third bout with bronchitis. The morning after I returned home, Rick had a major heart attack. Our eldest son, Chris, met me in the emergency room. I pulled my Bible from my bag and read from Psalm 121: "I lift up my eyes to the mountains—where does my help come from? My help comes from the Lord, the Maker of heaven and earth" (Psalm 121:1–2).

God miraculously spared Rick's life, and I am grateful every day. In September, it was "my turn," as I passed out in the ER, eventually having a hysterectomy and receiving seven units of blood. The first night in the hospital, when they couldn't get the bleeding to stop, I was afraid to go to sleep, because I thought I might bleed to death. I remembered another verse from Psalm 121: "He will not let your foot slip—he who watches over you will not slumber" (Psalm 121:3). Then I could close my eyes and sleep, because His eyes were on me. God wouldn't sleep. He would watch over my life.

My last secret is being diagnosed with breast cancer. Miraculously, after being prayed over, the cancer is gone. This is another blessing from a faithful God, for which I am grateful.

I was once a shy, shame-filled Dallas girl, but you have to get to the end of the book to discover all the victories God has in store.

Susan Lewis, *along with her husband, Rick, of forty-three years, own and operate the wonderful Christian book and gift store, Logos, at Snyder Plaza in Dallas, Texas. Susan is a wife, mother, and woman with a huge heart. She loves people and helping them find the words that can benefit them.*

Thoughts to Ponder
from Secrets

1. Our secrets are not hidden from God.

2. Don't tie your identity to anything but God.

3. Shame is an addiction that only God can heal.

What secrets bring you shame?

Nothing in all creation is hidden from God's sight. — Hebrews 4:13

Songs of My Heart
by Darryl Horn

Have you ever thought about how many kinds of music there are? Classical, Country, Contemporary Christian, Easy Listening, and Hard Rock. Then we have Rap, Reggae, Rock and Roll, Latin, Liturgical, Jazz, Blues, Bluegrass, Folk, Patriotic, Hip-Hop, Show Music—and more. Each is a favorite for someone.

Music stirs the soul, calms the nerves, and makes your toes tap and hands clap. It can fill you with joy or bring tears to your eyes. It can cause you to dance or put you to sleep.

Music touches your emotions. It can greatly impact you, reminding you of good times and bad. Words set to music may be the most powerful message of all.

Our lives are a musical score with high notes, low notes, sharp notes, and flat notes. Sometimes we are out of tune. But when we place our lives in the hands of the Master, Jesus, He can create beautiful music from all the "notes" of our lives.

My dad was a career Air Force man, so having grown up in a military family, I moved a lot during my younger years. Moving was always hard for me. I've lived in Arizona, Alabama, Kansas, Georgia, Texas, and even five years in England. I've lived in so many places, many songs are in my heart.

While most moves were ordinary, the worst move of my life was in my junior year in high school. My dad got "orders" to move from Wichita Falls, Texas, to Valdosta, Georgia, which wounded me deeply. My junior year in high school. Really? The song in my heart was low and mournful. For about three months, I was severely depressed. The chains of hopelessness were squeezing the life out of me. I did not want to live. Although I was seventeen, I didn't know how to ask for help. I often thought about ending my life, but thank God, I was ignorant about how to do it.

God knew I needed Him before I knew I needed Him.

So without personally knowing God and without knowing who was praying for me, God got me through it all. He blessed me with musical ability. I had been a percussionist since the fifth grade, active in band. When we moved to Georgia, I joined the varsity band. Through my involvement with band and new friendships,

God restored my desire to live.

God used music to set me free. I survived because of what He put inside me before I was born. He connected my inborn ability with a place for me to "shine." In my senior year, my band peers selected me as "Best Percussionist." Out of 515 graduating seniors, I ranked number 50, putting me in the top 10 percentile. God made my senior year in high school enjoyable, unique, and unforgettable. He made my music beautiful.

That fall, I attended Troy State University. My plan was to get a degree in biology so I could professionally work with snakes. During band camp, I met my wife. After four years dating, we married. Within the first few weeks of dating, we realized the importance of being connected to a church, so we sought a place to worship. The church had to be within walking distance of TSU, because neither one of us had a car.

We found a nearby church with a great college-campus outreach and became involved in the campus ministry. We heard the Word of God and associated with others who wanted to learn more about God, which was great. I learned simple life-exploding truths about this person called Jesus. I learned about His ground-breaking, life-changing, out-of-this-world message, which is called the Gospel—the "good news." In a world full of evil, ugliness, and all kinds of negative realities, God offers us good news. His name is Jesus. You might be wondering what truths were so life-changing.

The first truth I faced was about making right choices. You see, I thought, said, and did things that disappointed God, who cannot tolerate sin and doesn't want to be in its presence. His holiness won't allow it. And yet He desires to have a relationship with mankind. Our sin separates us from Him. Sin has a penalty, and the penalty must be paid. I had to come to grips with the truth that I was a sinner. It's a truth all of us must face, and sooner is better than later.

Another truth I had to face was that there wasn't anything in my power to solve my problem with sin. That's true for everyone, so the solution had to be provided for all humanity. Because of His great love, God provided the solution to our separation from Him by sending His Son, Jesus Christ, to pay the price for our sin. He, who never sinned, took our sins and paid the price by dying on the cross. His blood cleanses us from all sin and makes us acceptable to

God. When we accept His sacrifice, He accepts us. That's good news!

At age nineteen, I met my Lord and Savior Jesus Christ and decided to give my life to Him. Baptized in water, I grew in the things of God. My future wife was also baptized, and we began our spiritual journeys together.

I wish I could tell you that the reality of my new relationship with Jesus changed my attitude about snakes, but it didn't. My infatuation with those wicked creatures didn't end until decades later.

I was hired as a professional Reptile Keeper at the Dallas Zoo. I dropped out of college to work with snakes. I took time off work to attend my future wife's graduation, and then we got married. We had four children, all of them wonderful surprises—unplanned, but we wouldn't have had it any other way. They were "high notes" in our lives. The Bible says, "Children are a heritage from the Lord, offspring a reward from him" (Psalm 127:3).

Something life-changing happened at the zoo. While working in the snake house, I had a life-altering thought that caught me by surprise. Since childhood, I had focused on learning all I could about snakes and herpetology. The study of reptiles and amphibians was the primary focus of my life. Was I going to spend the next twenty to thirty years playing with these ridiculous ungodly snakes five days a week? The thought was absolutely demoralizing. Although it had been my life study, I needed to get out of that line of work.

The song in my heart went flat, and chains of depression again overwhelmed me. For several months, living became extremely difficult. Although I did not give any contemplation to suicide, my joy in living was gone. The music of my life drowned out the sweet chords of the Lord, for I had drifted. I had to find a new life in a new career. A few months later, I went from Reptile Keeper to encyclopedia salesman, to private security, and finally law enforcement.

My newfound occupation consumed my life. For some twenty-five years in a large metropolitan area, I worked the front-line of criminal street patrol, mostly at night. Contrary to fake news, police officers are not robots. They are human beings who feel pain, both emotionally and physically. They do a difficult job that grows more dangerous by the day.

During my time on the "thin blue line," there wasn't much I didn't see. Much of what I saw has been forgotten—suppressed memories that are difficult to recall. Some of the devilish memories are not the kinds of things you would want running around in your head. Allow me to share a few unforgettable memories.

- I watched someone die, knowing there was nothing I could do.
- Several times I delivered death notifications to people whose loved ones had committed suicide.
- I've been in the room when the doctor told a mom that a rival gang member had shot her son, and her teenager would not recover. That family's release of emotions is unforgettable.
- I have seen up-close the mangled and twisted bodies of people who were killed in motor vehicle accidents.

I eventually got to the place where I hated my job. One could not help being traumatized by the horrible memories. Unfortunately, I tended to ignore or hide the fact that I was really hurting on the inside. Years of trying to keep from being destroyed internally by the melancholy songs and the horrible world in which I worked sent my life into free-fall. I became unstable, mentally and emotionally. And then my family life began to fall apart.

- One of my adult children made a very poor choice and entered a disastrous marriage.
- My beloved mother-in-law unexpectedly passed away.
- The next year my dad unexpectedly died, the most traumatic situation of all.

I had a dream about my dad. When I woke up, he was heavy on my heart. In my mind I clearly heard these words: *You better go see your dad.* The Lord was trying to tell me something. I bought my plane ticket that day and saw my dad two weeks later. We had a good visit, but something was physically wrong. He had a lot of pain in his shoulder, and he hadn't seen a doctor. I thought the problem was a weight-lifting injury, since my dad was very athletic, even in his mid-sixties.

A couple months later, I made a second trip to see him, but this time I took my whole family. It was the last time all of us saw my dad alive. He had been a life-long smoker, and by the time we got him to the VA hospital, it was too late. The cancer had spread from his lungs through his shoulder and other parts of his body. Just over six weeks later, my dad, a thirty-year veteran of the United States Air Force, passed away. Today, it still hurts me that I didn't get to say goodbye.

I wasn't singing a happy song. My emotions sounded like a funeral dirge. The lowest notes on the piano don't come close to describing how I felt. After so many years on the front lines of law enforcement and the family tragedies, I found myself at an all-time low.

I drifted so far from God that I couldn't hear His voice among all the other voices trying to influence me. I was unstable in all my ways, so my life continued to deteriorate.

Desperate to feel better, I sought solace in my wife. Unfortunately, as I had drifted from God, we had grown too far apart from each other. We all have needs that can't be met by ourselves or anyone else. What I needed was a close, personal relationship with Jesus. Being unstable in my ways, I chose to leave the marriage. To her credit, she didn't want the divorce, but she graciously conceded.

Meanwhile, I was continuously experiencing all the lowest "notes" on the piano. I was flat, out of tune, and out of touch with God. My counselor's findings classified me as moderately to severely depressed. I was so used to the chains that I didn't recognize them. The counselor tried to help me, but I wasn't yet in a place to be helped.

And then, another trauma happened. Someone very close to me committed suicide, which had a devastating impact on me. I wasn't sure I could survive until I found a Survivor of Suicide support group. When I attended the first group meeting and heard stories of what other people had lived through, I knew I could endure it. But knowing that didn't mean I was stable. Facilitators tell survivors to avoid major decisions for two years. Again I didn't listen to counsel. My desperation was at a new "low." I wanted to "fix" myself, so I sought happiness and security in a new marriage.

My new wife and I had known each other for a few months. The marriage started off great and seemed to be all I thought it was going to be. However, the trials of relationship began. As things became unhinged, so did I. Instead of taking a couple years to heal, I carried my struggles into that marriage. We both did things to cause our marriage to spiral downward. I went deep into sin and made some of the worst choices of my life.

A phone call from a close friend saved my life. The Holy Spirit knew what I was dealing with and directed a longtime mentor and friend to encourage me, canceling the assignment by the enemy to destroy me. I retired early from law enforcement. A career spanning nearly two-and-a-half decades ended.

But God.

Seeing how far I had drifted from God, I knew it was time for repentance. My grievous sin had separated me from my God. Early in 2012, I got down on my face before God and poured out my heart. I repented of all my sin. I named them one-by-one and told God I was sorry. I acknowledged that I was wrong on so many levels, and I asked Him to forgive me. Just as He promised in the Bible, He forgave me and cleansed me from all unrighteousness (1 John 1:9). I also made a commitment to Him. For whatever time I had left on His planet, I would spend my days living for Him, His Kingdom, His purposes, and His glory. This was my new beginning. God gave me a new song with a new love for Him, for His Word, and for His plans for me.

In August 2012, God gave me a new place to live. I had visited Galveston before, but now the island city became my home. An apartment on the seawall provided the most spectacular sunrises, and God ministered to me. As the sun came up, I looked out on the Gulf of Mexico, and my bad memories seemed to fade.

I wanted to worship God with all my heart and grow in His ways, so God led me to a great church. My pastor's easy-going personality soothed my soul. Besides preaching fiery messages, he led the music ministry. His love of worshiping God was contagious, rubbing off on me. In the summer of 2013, he invited me to join the music ministry, and I served in that capacity until I moved from Galveston.

The pastor asked me to teach two different video-based thematic Bible studies: "The Purpose-Driven Life" and "You'll Get through This." In both series, the Spirit of God was pouring into me what I needed.

Something special happened when a visiting minister preached on Sunday morning. This man was gifted in speaking the direction of God into people's lives. After the service, he prayed for me and shared what was my new commission from the Lord. He did not know how God had been working in my heart about writing. After this prophetic word, God moved in me to develop a gift of writing, as well as to score beautiful music with words.

While I enjoy many types of music, I think the highest form of music is the worship of Almighty God. When we do that on a consistent basis from our hearts, chains can be broken. The more I praise God, the freer I am from the chains of anxiety, depression, and despair.

In sharing my story, I proclaim to you the reality of Jesus in my life. He saved me from my sins and gave me a wonderful new song. I have shared what He has done for me in the hope that you will be open to His love for you.

I will see you in Heaven!

Darryl Horn *served as a police officer over twenty-four years before retiring, and now diligently pursues his God-given call and passion to share the Gospel, encourage believers, and help build the Body of Christ by writing and publishing strong, biblically-based resources. He is an active Board Member of the Christian Writer's Workshop in Waco, Texas, and is also a member of Roaring Lambs' Roaring Writers. A musician of many years early in life, he now loves to sing only for the Lord Almighty. Darryl can be reached at* **DarryLHornWrites@gmail.com**.

Thoughts to Ponder
from Songs of My Heart

1. God knows we need Him before we know we need Him.

2. God can put a new song in your heart.

3. With God, you can make beautiful music together.

What is the theme song of your life?

Always giving thanks to God the Father for everything, in the name of our Lord Jesus Christ. — Ephesians 5:20

Who's My Father?

by Debbie Buffone

I want to ask you two questions. Does your life have meaning? Are you a happy person? The reason I ask you is because I now know my life has meaning. My friends always say I am one of the happiest persons they've ever met. My life is full of joy, and I praise God every day for the life He has given me. I get sad and cry myself to sleep sometimes. I complain more than I should, and I let myself be disappointed. I believe all this is part of being human and living in a broken world.

Before I tell you the real reason for my happiness and the joyful approach I have to my meaningful life, I'd like to introduce you to a young woman. She left her parents' house in her teens, only to find herself surrounded by drugs and sexual promiscuity. Her name is Shoshana Lines. Knowing that her Jewish heritage would not go well with her job position, she changed her name to Brigitte Lines. She was a prostitute. She had many children with different fathers and raised those children to be free and to live reckless lives. Brigitte then met the youngest son of a family of Italian immigrants, and they had a long relationship.

He was the black sheep of his family and was involved in drugs, both in using and trafficking. Brigitte found herself pregnant by this young man, and they both decided to terminate the senseless pregnancy. She tried to abort the baby three times, but because of life-threatening reasons, she had to let the pregnancy continue to full-term. When she was six months into the pregnancy, she had an argument with the father of the baby, and he pushed her from a second-floor balcony. She was rushed to the hospital, and he was arrested.

Three months after this episode, I was born.

In the Bible, John 10:10 says, "The thief comes only to steal and kill and destroy; I [Jesus] have come that they may have life, and have it to the full."

I possess the full and abundant life promised in the Bible. For some reason, the enemy of our lives tried to stop me from being born, but God Himself provided a safe way for me to be here, and I praise Him every day for His grace and love toward me.

I don't know the exact day I was born. Nobody paid attention to that. There's no record of the day, the year, or even the place, but I know God was there the day I was conceived. Another passage in the Bible makes me believe this. Psalms 22:10 says, "From birth I was cast on you; from my mother's womb you have been my God."

We don't have any memory of the time we spent in our mother's wombs. However, I still like to imagine what it was like while growing there. I was so close to my mother. I needed her with every fiber of my being. So I believe the first person I wanted to see when I was born was the owner of that beautiful heartbeat, my mother. But when I was born, she didn't want me. She didn't keep me. Someone was hired to take me home and care for me. Later, my mother would decide what to do with me. So I waited for my mommy to come back.

I grew up with different families, and a few times someone wanted to adopt me. Because nobody could find my biological parents and because I never legally belonged to anyone, adoption was impossible. Life wasn't easy, because as I was growing up I was also asking questions like, *Do I have a mother and a father? Why do I look different? Why don't I have a family or a mommy and a daddy like my friends do?*

I used to look at strangers and dream about the possibility of them being my long-lost parents. Any woman could have been my mother. Any man could have been my father. I wanted to know what the love and care of a mom looked like. I needed to experience the comfort and protection that only a father can give to a little girl. All I had, though, was this empty space, this feeling of rejection and abandonment taking root and growing bigger inside me. My life had no meaning at all.

One time, I noticed that my friend's hands looked like her mother's hands. I couldn't tell if my hands looked like my mother's hands, but I knew for sure that my hands looked just like God's hands. That's because I was fearfully and wonderfully created by Him, made in His image. God impressed those things in my heart even before I was old enough to read it in the Bible. What an amazing God!

When I was almost eleven years old, my mother came back. I remember that day vividly. I had waited so long for that day and now she was right there in front of me. She was so beautiful, but so cold. There weren't any hugs or holding me on her lap. She only came to take care of business. She owed some money to the family. She meticulously checked me and exchanged some words with the adults in the room. I remember finding courage to say, "I go to church."

"What a shame," she said. "What have they done to you? Did they brainwash you?"

She took me to the hotel where she was staying with my oldest half-sister. She sat me down at a table and told me she was going to see my future. She laid on a table some cards with funny figures on them. She was a tarot card reader. What she didn't know was that my future had already been laid out by God, even before I was born.

During our stay at the hotel, I played at the pool all day. I could pick up the phone and order all the ice cream I wanted. My mother had come back to let me live with her, to belong to her. She would take care of me and protect me until I was old enough to take care of myself. Life had been so hard without her by my side, but now the past was the past and I could finally think of my future with my mother. It was not just a dream. It was happening.

After a long day playing in the pool, I was in the elevator with my mother and half-sister, returning from the restaurant downstairs. My mother asked if I wanted to get into my bathing suit and go back to the pool to play with her friend. I had to control myself to not scream an excitedly loud yes. Of course I wanted to go back to the pool at night. I had never done that before. We got back in our room, and I put on my bathing suit. I noticed my mom and half-sister arguing over something, or someone—over me.

My mother had sold me to a man during the day at the pool, and he had already given her a down payment. He would give the rest of the money to my mother when she delivered me to him. My half-sister grabbed me and told my mother she would not let her do that to me. I was just a child, she said, and she forced my mother out of her room. We all moved out of the hotel that night. They took me back to the same people she had hired to take care of me, and I never saw her again. Once again, the angels of God were sent to protect me. What a mighty God!

Even though my dream of having a loving mother was gone, I still had the dream of having a father. I needed to belong. So as I was growing older, I found out more about him. With the information I had gathered in the years since my mother left, I finally looked for him.

When I boldly ventured to my father's workplace, I was in junior high. I was about to go on a very exciting adventure into high school, and now I'd be reaching another goal in life by finding my daddy.

I met the most handsome man of my life. He was my hero, my prince. He was the rescuer I had dreamed of. My father. My daddy. From that day on, I would have a family. My father was married and had two daughters. So I now had two sisters, a father, and a stepmother. Life could not have been so complete. I belonged to a real family. My father was a loving daddy. He would pick me up at school every Friday so I could spend the weekends with him and my sisters until I finished the year at school. Three months had passed since I met my beautiful father for the first time. Oh, how happy and full of life I was!

One day, right before Christmas, my father came to get me at school, but this time he took me home and sexually abused me. I was devastated, scared, and confused. I reached out to my stepmother for answers and comfort, but that night she took turns with my father to again abuse me.

Early in the morning, I gathered some of my schoolbooks. With only what I was wearing, I left their house and began planning how to end my life. I didn't go through with my plans. God gave me strength to rise above this dreadful time.

I never saw my father again. He never called and never reached out to me. I was left without answers and was once again alone. But God was still with me. Yes. God has always been my strong tower and my shelter. He is my everything.

Let's fast-forward to five years ago. I made a trip to Brazil to see friends and meet family members for the first time. During this trip, I promised myself I would not accept any speaking engagements, but God had other plans. I accepted an invitation to speak at a local church and share my testimony. I had never been to that church and only knew a couple friends there.

As I spoke, I felt that I had to tell about the day my mother took me to the hotel, how I spent the day at the pool, how my wet feet slipped on the stairs. I fell, and a nice man helped pick me up. I was ashamed to tell everyone that my own mother had sold me as a sex slave to a man when I was a little girl. What happened next can only be explained by the Holy Spirit of God.

After I finished speaking, the service was over, and I was visiting with friends. I heard the pastor call my name and walk toward me. He was crying and had his arm around another man who was also crying. He told everyone standing there, "Debbie, this is so amazing. You need to meet this man."

When the man composed himself, he told us why he was crying. He said, "I am the man who bought you! I am sorry. I was young and a rebel. I was living at that hotel because my wealthy family couldn't keep up with all the problems I had caused them. I remember the details of you as a little girl, playing at the pool. I remember how you fell, and I ran to catch you. What you didn't know is that I had already paid your mother for you. She never delivered you that night, and she disappeared with the money. I got older, married, and had children of my own, but I never quite forgot you. One day, I accepted Christ as my Savior, but the guilt I had in my heart came back to haunt me for many years. I was perverted, a pedophile, and never forgave myself. Today, you are here, and I am asking you to forgive me."

All of us were in shock and crying. I hugged that man and told him, "I forgive you." What a mighty God we serve! That man, plagued by a guilty conscience, was at church that very day to see the same little girl he once bought as a sex slave, who was now a woman who loved the Lord, the same Lord Jesus who had saved him from his past. And now he was given the opportunity of a lifetime to redeem himself and be forgiven.

Do you see why I say my life has joy and meaning? Life has never given me reasons to believe it, but Jesus is the reason I live. I have never belonged to anyone. I have never had a real family to love me unconditionally, but God has provided me with the love and care of a wonderful family of friends wherever I go. It has not been easy on my own. Sometimes I need someone to walk alongside me, to guide me and answer my questions. Sometimes God puts beautiful people in front of me to do just that. At other times, He gives me dreams and speaks to me through His Word, the Bible.

I still climb onto His lap when I need a hug. He is a loving Father, and He wipes away my tears. After I have fallen asleep on His lap, I always wake up feeling better.

My life has meaning, and the meaning of my life is Jesus. Would you like to have a whole and meaningful life too? Invite Jesus to be part of it, and you will never be the same. I know.

I am alive and well because of Him!

Debbie Buffone is originally from Brazil, but now works as Governess for a family in Plano, Texas. She is a writer and speaker and is active at her Messianic Synagogue, Beth Sar Shalom. She is also a faithful volunteer at Roaring Lambs Ministries.

Thoughts to Ponder
from Who's My Father?

1. It doesn't matter who birthed you once you are a child of God.

2. Life has no coincidence, only a God incident.

3. Even when sadness wants to overtake us, God can infuse us with joy.

How have you found joy despite tragedy?

Weeping may stay for the night,
but rejoicing comes in the morning. — Psalm 30:5

A Dream Come True

by Geni Manning

Have you ever had a childhood dream that wouldn't go away?

During the summer after fifth grade, a friend asked me to join her as a "Peewee" cheerleader for her brother's football team. It was great fun and for the first time, I received attention and felt I belonged. More than that, I got the bug to be a cheerleader—a dream that quickly consumed me.

I still had two more years in grade school, but that didn't stop me from training to realize my dream. In my spare time, I practiced my cheers, jumps, and splits. I pretended to be the cheerleader I expected to become in junior high. In my little working-class neighborhood in Hurst, Texas, cheerleading was a big deal.

My three sisters and I were one year apart in age, and I was the youngest—a fact that made for interesting stories with our teachers and friends. Affectionately known as the "McKelvey Girls," we were well known in our small town.

Growing up wasn't easy for any of us, but as the youngest, I seemed to have a harder time making my way. I grew up in a broken home. My mother and father divorced when I was eighteen months old, and I saw my dad only twice as a child. On her own, Mom had difficulty supporting us. The poverty, hardship, and stress made her a bitter woman. She never wasted an opportunity to tell us how worthless our father was. No one wants to hear negativity about her dad—especially an impressionable young girl.

My sisters were pretty and popular. They had a lot of friends and were always being chosen or nominated for something in school, like "Most Beautiful," "Homecoming Queen," or "School Favorite." And then there was me. In my mind, I was the "ugly duckling," the "black sheep," and "the girl who was never good enough."

From an early age, I felt the absence of parental love and acceptance. Feelings of being overlooked, forgotten, and undervalued left me empty. I desperately wanted to be loved and acknowledged. I felt alone in a house full of people, and no matter how hard I tried, I could never keep up with my sisters.

The older McKelvey girls were talented athletes and dancers, known by everyone in town. They held significant positions on the high school drill team.

When I finally got to junior high, I was obsessed with trying out for the cheerleading team, certain that my Peewee experience and hard work would pay off. At last, I could make my perpetually disapproving mom proud and show my sisters that I also mattered.

However, my dream was derailed when I received a C in conduct on my report card, a grade that disqualified me from tryouts. I panicked and pleaded with my teacher.

"Please, Mr. Singletary, I'm sorry for being any trouble. I promise to do better. Really, I will. But I just have to try out for the team. Please!" I begged for mercy, and my sincere apology did the trick. This kind teacher gave me a second chance and changed my grade to a B so I could try out.

"Thank you," I shouted as I bolted out of the room. "I won't let you down."

Elated, I shared the exciting news with someone I thought was a close friend. "I'll be able to try out after all," I said.

My friend seemed genuinely happy for me.

However, that wasn't the case. The next day, I discovered that she had complained to the principal, who made Mr. Singletary change my grade back. I was stunned. I was thirteen years old, and this was the first time I had experienced the acute pain of betrayal. I thought we were friends. I couldn't understand how—or why—she could go behind my back and hurt me. It was inconceivable.

My childhood dream was shattered, and I lost all interest in school and the people in it. Desperate to find acceptance and a deeper meaning in life, I looked for other things to replace the dream that had consumed me for so many years.

This was the beginning of a dark season of poor choices, not the least of which was my decision to quit school and leave home as a teenager. I eventually got my driver's license, bought a car, obtained my GED, and enrolled in a business college. Meanwhile, I worked in meaningless, dead-end part-time jobs.

I missed out on high school entirely. I never experienced homecoming, the prom, or what it would be like to follow in my sisters' impressive footsteps. Most of all, I missed out on my dream to be a school cheerleader. The next four years were difficult, but I had a strong will. Somehow, I would survive.

My sisters graduated from high school and were twenty, twenty-one, and twenty-two years old. Vicci taught dance and aerobic classes at Tarrant County Junior College. Robin moved to attend a Bible college in California. Cyndi was a flight attendant for Braniff Airlines.

At nineteen, I wanted to be a flight attendant and travel the world too. I had just confirmed interviews with several major airlines when Cyndi called with an unusual invitation.

"Geni, the Cowboys are having tryouts for next season's cheerleading squad. I'm going to give it a shot, and I want you to come with me."

What? Cyndi's invitation surprised me, but she was clearly excited.

"Tex is really pumped-up. He has awesome new ideas—a vision to take the Dallas Cowboy cheerleaders to a level no one has seen before in professional football. Pete thinks it's going to be incredible. Come on, you have to go with me."

The Tex she mentioned was Tex Schramm, president and general manager of the team, and Pete was the fellow Cyndi was dating, who was Tex's good friend. This distinction afforded them the opportunity to watch Cowboy games with Schramm in his VIP box—a perk Cyndi loved. Watching the cheerleaders perform brought back memories from her high school drill team days.

The Dallas Cowboys Cheerleaders premiered in 1972 as the first official professional cheerleaders in history. Sophisticated jazz dancing blended with beauty was brought to a football field.

Before then, the dancers on the sidelines were high school students from the DFW area, teenage girls and boys, called the *CowBelles & Beaux.* They cheered the Cowboys all the way to their 1971 Super Bowl Championship, their last year on the sidelines.

Cyndi continued to recruit me. "Come on, Geni. I know you always wanted to be a cheerleader. This is your chance. The Cowboys just won the Super Bowl. Next season, we'll get to cheer for the World Champions. Trust me, the new and improved Dallas Cowboys Cheerleaders are going to be a really big thing."

Clearly, she was excited about the tryouts, but I thought her assessment of the potential was a bit exaggerated. After all, how "really big" could a team of football cheerleaders get?

I had long ago buried my schoolgirl dream and was focused on how to make a living as an adult. "Cyndi, I need to get a *real* job. I don't have time to play."

Relentless, Cyndi about drove me crazy.

I might have been strong-willed, but I was shy. After listening to her explain how the tryouts would work, I decided a verbal interview might be good practice for my interviews with the airlines. For the dancing part, I thought I had a 50/50 chance of not falling flat on my face.

Over 2,000 girls applied. Because of the huge turnout, auditions were split into several days. Cyndi and I were separated. "At least you won't see me make a fool of myself," I said to her.

From the moment I showed up at the tryouts, I knew I was way out of my league. All the girls were gorgeous, dressed like fashion models. My outfit from K-Mart looked small town.

"Okay, ladies," the director said. "For this first stage, we're going to call you up four at a time. Tell us a little about yourself, and then we'll ask you to dance."

The music was high-energy disco, and the judges wanted to see if we had any natural rhythm. I felt reasonably comfortable with my ability for that part. The verbal interview concerned me, and rightfully so. I bombed miserably. Somehow, I managed to get through the day, completely embarrassed that I had even tried.

"Thank you, ladies," the director said. "We'll contact you by mail and let you know if you did or didn't make the cut."

Cyndi believed she had aced the entire thing, certain she would be asked back.

"Well, there's no way I'll be asked back," I said to a girl sitting next to me. "That was brutal. I don't know how I let myself be talked into this." Not wanting to repeat this agony, I was perfectly fine with not being asked back.

I'm only here to practice for my interviews for the airlines—I'm going to be a flight attendant. I dismissed the painful experience from my mind.

A week later, I was dumbfounded. A letter from the Cowboys' office invited me back for the semi-finals. Certain that Cyndi had received her letter as well, I called to share my unexpected news.

"Cyndi, they asked me back. Can you believe it? I can't believe it. It's probably because of you, and they felt sorry for me. But it is kind of cool. What are you going to wear? What date did they give you to come back? I hope we aren't separated again—maybe we can ride together." I was rambling like a crazy person when I realized that Cyndi was unusually quiet. "You got your letter too, right?"

"Yes, I got it, but they didn't ask me to come back."

I felt bad for Cyndi. She knew the Cowboys president and general manager and was dating his best friend. And she was the one with all the experience from her years on the drill team.

A part of me was excited. I wouldn't go past the semifinals. They were sure to see how wrong I was for their team, but the experience was amazing. This would give me another chance to practice my interviews with the airlines.

At the semifinal callback, we were asked to do a series of high kicks and splits.

Seriously?

I hadn't done splits since junior high, and I never had a reason to do high kicks.

I nailed both the splits and the high kicks. Clearly a miracle.

Later that day, they taught us a dance routine to see if we could learn it quickly. I made it through my performance, but I couldn't hold a candle to the other girls in the lineup. They were awesome. The majority had been cheerleaders or were on a drill team from junior high to college. Most of them had been taking dance lessons since grade school.

It was over.

After a week, another letter arrived. To my surprise, I was again invited back. Why was God being so cruel, teasing me this way? God wasn't vengeful. He had a plan for me. I just couldn't figure out what it was. Why was He making me go through all this?

We were nearing the official end of the road. This was the last invitation—the finals. There would be no more letters, no more waiting, no more chances. A small group of incredibly lucky young women would become the Dallas Cowboys Cheerleaders.

What should have been excitement quickly turned to panic when I read that I must have my own music and dance routine. I wasn't sure how I had managed to fool the judges so far, but this was most definitely the end of the road. There was no way I could choreograph a professional dance routine.

"Geni, we can do this," my oldest sister, Vicci, said. "I've got a ton of ideas."

She had been a lieutenant on the high school drill team and choreographed several trophy-winning dances for their squad.

Using the theme song from the TV show *Hawaii Five-O*, she created a great routine with lots of jazz and sass—something entirely out of my comfort zone. We practiced every waking moment until the finals.

On that all-important day, I surprised myself. I never thought I could be bold enough to do something like this, but I pulled off what I thought was a spunky, snazzy routine. My performance was still pale compared to the other girls, who were like something out of an MGM casting call. One phenomenal dance routine after another left many of the judges applauding wildly. After everyone had danced, the judges asked us a few more questions and had us complete some final exercises.

"Thank you, ladies," the director said. "It's been a long day, and you've all done an excellent job. Now it's time for us to make some important decisions. If you'll have a seat, we will make the announcements soon."

As we sat in the swanky Cowboys Club overlooking the stadium, nervous anticipation blew in like a hot summer breeze. This would be the end of the line for many of us.

For only a few minutes, the five judges huddled, comparing photographs, score sheets, and notes.

"Ladies," the director said, "instead of your names, we're going to call out your competition numbers. When you hear your number, please join us down here."

Each time a number was called, people in the crowd screamed, and a girl ran to the front, something like *The Price Is Right* game show. I wasn't going to make the final cut, and I was okay with that. We all seemed to be genuinely excited for every winner.

About three quarters of the way through the announcements, a number was called, but no one screamed. We looked to see who the next Dallas Cowboys Cheerleader was, but no one jumped up. No one answered the second and third call. What had happened to girl #192? That someone had come so far and left before hearing the good news was inconceivable.

"Ladies," the judge shouted, "is Geni McKelvey here?"

I snapped to stunned attention when I realized they had been calling *my* number.

Were they really calling me? I slowly stood with my hand over my mouth in total disbelief. As my fellow contestants clapped, a judge saw me and shouted, "Yes, you. Come on down."

As I made my way out of the row and walked to the front, a lifetime of disappointment passed before my eyes. I remembered when my cheerleading dream was yanked from my grasp and wondered if this too could be a cruel joke.

Immediately after the last girl was announced, the media rushed in with their film and camera crews. The room was electrified. Every local station major network was there, as well as national magazines like *People*, *Redbook*, and *Life*. Caught up in the frenzy of activity, I realized that Cyndi was right. This was a very big deal—and I was part of it. Until then, I had been clueless about its significance. I didn't know how much the forward-thinking Tex had been strategically promoting his plans for this new squad. I had no idea how much America loved football, especially the Dallas Cowboys.

They say everything is big in Texas, and Tex Schramm's vision was no exception. When he first introduced the world to the Dallas Cowboys Cheerleaders in 1972, his timing was right for establishing a football tradition of a glamorous, choreographed squad of accomplished female dancers as sideline cheerleaders.

As the Cowboys were preparing to defend their World Championship title in 1978, the next-generation vision Tex had for his cheerleaders was getting much bigger. Under the direction of Suzanne Mitchell, a woman who would become one of the most important, yet one of the most overlooked women in the NFL, the brilliant plan was executed.

I still wasn't sure how it happened, but I was now part of this growing vision.

Driving home that evening, I was filled with anticipation of how my life would change. Although jubilant, I was still trying to wrap my head around what had just happened. We went from 2,000 girls to 36. How could I have pulled that off?

Then it dawned on me, and the tears flowed. *You didn't make this happen, Geni. It was a miracle gift from God—a dream He fulfilled.*

We trained all summer, and when the 1977–78 NFL season kicked off, we began a new chapter in cheerleader history. All 65,000 eyes were on us as we danced into Texas Stadium, wearing our star-spangled uniforms, cowboy boots, and smiles—introduced as "America's Sweethearts." Often imitated, but never equaled, we were The Dallas Cowboys Cheerleaders.

All thirty-six cheerleaders became instant celebrities. Remember, being a cheerleader in my little home town was a big deal. So you can imagine how much bigger the national spotlight was.

When I tried out, I had no idea what direction my life would take. Of course, God knew. My dream had been crushed as a schoolgirl, but God fulfilled my childhood dream in a much bigger and better way.

The new-and-improved Dallas Cowboys Cheerleaders made their mark on history. Everywhere we turned, new doors opened. The Dallas Cowboys Cheerleader poster debuted, an iconic image that became a cultural phenomenon. It turned out to be the hottest selling piece of memorabilia in the team's history, a best-seller across the nation, rivaling the famous Farrah Fawcett poster. The first calendar followed. Our photos appeared on decks of playing cards and Frisbees. There were even cheerleader dolls. Then we started USO tours, entertaining military troops far away.

As the Dallas Cowboys Cheerleaders success grew, America's Sweethearts soon received world recognition. We traveled to Tokyo and performed at the Mirage Bowl. Over that two-week tour, we were on numerous TV talk shows and made several commercials. Our squad led one of the biggest parades in Tokyo history. We were treated like celebrities. Everywhere we went, we received a gift. It was amazing.

Back in the US, we appeared on television programs like the *Love Boat*, the *Bob Hope Show*, the *Oakridge Boys*, the *Osmond Brothers Special*, and NBC's *Rock-n-Roll Sports Classic*. The Dallas Cowboys Cheerleaders produced a one-hour TV special: *The 36 Most Beautiful Ladies in Texas* and a made-for-TV movie called *The Dallas Cowboys Cheerleaders*, starring Bert Convey and Jane Seymour. We made a Faberge commercial and were featured in *Esquire* magazine. Every week, the Cowboys highlighted one cheerleader in the *Cowboys Weekly* magazine and soon realized that our popularity demanded our own magazine called the *Dallas Cowboys Cheerleaders*. The book included pictures and bios of all cheerleaders, as well as action pictures from the sidelines, tryouts, and USO tours.

All of us were given incredible opportunities to represent the

Cowboys, making special appearances across the nation. To prepare, we attended an eight-week course at the Dale Carnegie Institute, participating in the classic *How to Win Friends and Influence People* program.

If all that wasn't enough, we cheered at the Super Bowl in Miami to defend our championship title. Unfortunately, we lost in the last five seconds of the game. Despite the loss, the year was truly unforgettable. My dream had come true.

The Dallas Cowboys Cheerleaders became the darlings of the National Football League and a major commodity for the Cowboys. For me, however, the experience was far more personal.

After a heartbreaking childhood, I experienced a series of miracles and second chances that could only be explained as gifts from God. Even when I felt unworthy and unloved, He was working behind the scenes to develop me into something special He could use. The absence of an earthly father may have left a hole in my heart, but my heavenly Father filled it completely. My years as a poor little troubled girl with an uncertain future did not go unnoticed by God. In my darkest moments, He cultivated in me the tools I would need to be part of an international platform that allowed amazing opportunities to share my faith.

And so it was that I fumbled into the role of a Dallas Cowboys cheerleader. For that, I give all the glory, honor, and praise to the One who planned it all.

Dreams are gifts that God gives to us—fulfilled in His time—not ours. And rest assured, these heavenly gifts are grand displays of the love our Father has for us.

Geni Manning — *After a heartbreaking childhood, and through a series of miracles and second chances, Geni fumbled into the role of a Dallas Cowboys Cheerleader at the peak of their fame. She was privileged to be part of the celebrated "America's Sweethearts." However, behind the glamour and stardom, Geni continued to struggle with devastating heartaches, such as failed relationships, broken marriages, the loss of a child, and a family legacy. Geni is now a successful real estate agent in the Dallas/Fort Worth metroplex and is working on a book,* Sixty and Single.

Thoughts to Ponder

from A Dream Come True

1. Dreams really can come true.

2. Delayed dreams have a purpose.

3. God puts desires in our hearts based on what He knows will happen.

> ## **What dreams has God put in your heart?**

Take delight in the Lord, and he will give you the desires of your heart — Psalm 37:4

Are You Ready for the Test?
by Michelle Ruddell

Have you ever taken a test you were unprepared for? Maybe you hadn't studied enough. Possibly the material was too difficult. Perhaps the test was a surprise, like a pop quiz. I faced such a test once. I had just finished my first year of teaching. The alternative high school where I taught was undergoing a reorganization. *We would love to have you continue teaching here, but to do that we need you to get certified in math.* The principal's words echoed in my brain.

A few days later, I sat in an auditorium filled with other soon-to-be math teachers. As I looked around the room, I felt out of place and insecure. I just *knew* that all those people were brilliant scholars who could easily ace this test. I imagined they could see "not a math teacher" stamped across my forehead.

I opened my test booklet. Some problems were easy, and I answered them quickly. Others were more difficult. I worked as far as I could and took an educated guess. Then I turned a page and nearly laughed out loud. I had never seen these symbols before. I was overwhelmed. I stared at the fancy graphing calculator I had borrowed from a friend. I knew how to use it to figure out how many questions I could miss and still pass. I had not, however, spent enough time working with this device to know how to access more-advanced features that would have been very useful.

This test made me aware of a need. To be successful on this test, I needed help. In the days that followed, I was tutored by people who knew a lot about math. I studied, and I practiced. I learned how to use that fancy calculator. After several months and a few more attempts, I passed the test. Through that experience, I learned to relate to my students who struggle. I identify with those who are overwhelmed and insecure. I can guide them and help them build their confidence.

Life has presented me with other challenges like the math test I took that day. For some of the tests, I am unprepared. Sometimes the difficulties are due to my own choices. In most situations, the experience is difficult. Many of life's exams come unannounced, like the dreaded pop quiz. However, because of the challenges, I have experienced three significant life tests that have made me aware of a need. Each of these events has taught me an important truth.

One test I was unprepared for happened in December 1992. It was an exciting day. My husband, my five-year-old son, and I were preparing to celebrate our first Christmas as a family reconciled after divorce. We had remarried in August of that year, and we were expecting a baby. Our plans included a trip to Lubbock, about an hour away, to finish shopping. On the way, a driver on the opposite side of the highway lost control on the slippery road. His car crossed the median and hit us head-on.

I do not recall everything that happened. But vivid sights and sounds from the accident are forever etched in my mind. I was anxious as I drifted in and out of consciousness in the ambulance. I worried about my son, Matthew, who was taken in another ambulance to a different hospital. I worried that the medical professionals would unknowingly give me treatment or medication, harming my unborn baby.

At the hospital, I stared at the ceiling from the gurney. I was in a neck brace and on a back board. The doctors in the room said, "Your husband is in critical condition. His injuries are extensive. We are doing all we can to save his life."

My parents entered the room. My mother was crying. She told me that Matthew had not survived. The news took my breath away, as if the world had stopped turning. How could this be? Just this morning, Matthew was running up and down the driveway in his snow boots, sliding down the tiny incline to the street. Just this morning, he stopped abruptly on his run through the house, wrapped his arms around me, and said, "I love you, Mom."

This unannounced test was too difficult. I wasn't prepared. I was devastated. I was desperate for someone to tell me it wasn't true. Words filled with grief escaped my mouth: "Not my baby!"

My husband was clinging to life but had told the doctors he didn't want to live if Matthew didn't make it. My son, my world as I had treasured it, was gone. The doctors said my unborn baby's heartbeat was strong, but I doubted that such a fragile being could survive the trauma. I cried out to God in desperation and heartbreak. I needed His help to go on in this unfamiliar new reality.

My cry for help was heard. In the days and weeks after the

wreck, I put one foot in front of the other. I breathed in, and I breathed out. Minute by minute, day by day, I asked God for help. My husband came home after more than two months in the hospital. He had significant physical injuries, and he was searching for a way to deal with Matthew's death. In May, our beautiful, healthy daughter was born—the first of many times I experienced pure joy alongside deep sorrow.

A few days after my son's funeral, I sat at my parents' kitchen table with my mom, her neighbor, and some other women. I don't remember much of the conversation, but at one point the neighbor looked me in the eye and said, "You will never be happy again." I knew this woman had lost a son years ago. I also knew her to be generally grumpy and unhappy. I excused myself from the table and ducked into the nearest bedroom. When you are pregnant and have just buried your child, you can do or say just about anything, and no one will question you. I collapsed into a chair in my parents' bedroom.

"I don't want to be like that," I cried out to God. "This is hard, and it hurts. I miss my son, but I want to be happy again."

For a long time, the memory of the neighbor's words made me angry. How dare she say something like that to a newly grieving mother? As time passed, there were minutes, hours, and days where I really *wanted* to be bitter. I wanted to feel sorry for myself. I wanted everyone around me to know how unfair life was and how deeply I hurt. Then I remembered her words. And I remembered my prayer.

I chose to be happy through the sadness.

Difficult and unannounced, this test was excruciating and revealed my need for God. I was unprepared. Without God, I would be unable to cope with the grief of losing my child. What would life be like without my son?

I learned that God's love is unconditional. As a nine-year-old child, I had invited Jesus into my life. I understood that He wanted to be part of my life. I knew He came to Earth, that He died to forgive us, and that He rose again. As I grew, my understanding of my relationship with Him was based on being good. I did my best to follow the rules. I focused on *dos* and *don'ts*.

When I was nineteen, I found myself in an environment where people didn't believe or behave like me. There were choices and actions that I was tempted to try. In this environment, I met the man who would become my husband. I walked willingly into things that were on the list of *don'ts*. I had gone far away from everything I had been taught. I was ashamed. After all I had done, I felt like there was no way back for me.

At Matthew's death when I cried out to God, He answered my cry for help. He comforted me and helped me function in my grief. I learned from this test that God is present. He heard me when I called to Him, and I realized that His love is unconditional. I had a new understanding of what it meant for God to send His Son to die for me.

After the wreck, life was difficult. While working through grief, I was also living with a husband who was undergoing a difficult physical and emotional recovery. The addiction that had gripped him in the past returned with a vengeance. The physical violence that had never completely been absent from our marriage escalated to the point that I feared for my life. I wasn't sure what the future held for me. I was now the mother of two daughters, ages three and one. I felt rejected, hopeless, and helpless. I didn't see a way out. I knew God loved me, but this test was a result of my own choices. Like students who fail because they didn't study, I was in the middle of a difficult test, because I had chosen to marry this man—again.

One day, my daughter, who was now three, looked up at me. "Is my daddy going to kill you?"

This test was one I couldn't pass on my own. I needed help. I lacked the skills and resources that this challenge required. That night, after everyone else was asleep, I knelt in front of the couch and begged God's forgiveness. I admitted to Him that I had not followed His plan for my life. I pleaded for guidance and clear direction on what to do. I went to sleep with an unfamiliar peace. I trusted God to hear and answer my prayer.

In the following weeks, I looked for reasons to stay. I remembered the famous advice columnist's words: "Are you better off with him or without him?" As I observed all our day-to-day interactions, I didn't see one thing I could consider a reason to stay. I asked God to show me when and how I could get out of this life-threatening marriage.

On Easter Sunday morning, I drew the wrath of my husband

because I woke him. When the one-sided fight was over, something was different. On most occasions, he calmed down afterward, but not this time. I wondered if there was another bout coming. We went into the kitchen to begin cooking. The sanity amidst the insanity was that we were expecting guests for Easter lunch.

My husband was the boss in the kitchen. He barked orders, and I did my best to comply. When I didn't meet one demand soon enough, he turned, scowling, and raised the spatula in his hand. In that instant, I knew it was time to leave. I can't tell you what was different about that moment, but I had no doubt that *this was the time*.

I placed the platter I was holding on the counter. I turned and walked through the living room and out the front door. I considered raising the garage door to get my van but decided against it. I was afraid the sound of the door being raised would alert my husband of my attempt to leave. I chose to walk instead.

A convenience store was about half a mile from the house. I went in and bought a soft drink. I rested a minute, looking over my shoulder, expecting to be chased down any second. I had attempted to leave on several other occasions. My husband had always forced me, or convinced me, to come back. So far, I had not been followed.

I walked from the store to the courthouse, where I sat on the steps and contemplated my situation. I wanted to be sure before I went into the sheriff's office and filed a complaint. I worked around law enforcement professionals and recognized that most women who file on their abusers come in the next day and withdraw the complaint. I didn't want to follow that pattern. If I went through with this, I wanted it to be for good.

Sitting on the courthouse steps on Easter Sunday, I knew my world was about to change. I asked God for help. He was answering. The feeling was surreal. I went in and filed the complaint. My husband was arrested. My sister-in-law and her boyfriend stayed at the house with my daughters. When I returned home, we continued a somewhat subdued Easter celebration, including hiding eggs for the girls.

I felt a new freedom.

My husband's friend bailed him out the next day. I heard the same apologies I had heard before. My husband played the perfect

110

gentleman, bringing gifts, making promises, and even agreeing to marriage counseling. This was an attempt to get me to drop the complaint and keep him out of jail. I had a new, unfamiliar strength to resist his ploys. The charges remained. Because he was on parole for previous offenses, he was arrested and sent to prison.

My daughters and I were free.

I felt like this difficult test was my fault, a result of my bad choices. This test made me aware of my need for a relationship with God. I cried out to Him, and He answered. He provided a way out. He provided strength to follow through with my decision. I felt confident and assured that God was for me. I wanted to know Him better.

In the next few years, I studied God's Word. I found people who knew more about Him than I did and learned from them. I learned to depend on Him daily and grew closer to Him. I was unaware that everything I was learning was preparing me for another test.

When my daughter was fifteen, she started having some scary health issues. My active teenager, who had just made the varsity tennis team, had severe pains in her neck. The doctors weren't sure what was causing them. The pains affected her back, arms, and legs. Rest didn't help. Medicine didn't help. Doctors didn't know what to do. Some told us it was "all in her head."

After months of searching for answers, a neurologist determined what was causing my daughter's trouble. "She has dystonia," he said, "a movement disorder similar to Parkinson's Disease. We can treat the symptoms, but there is no cure. We are not sure how far the symptoms will progress."

I was overwhelmed. I hurt for my daughter. I was angry. I told God, "She's been through enough. This is not fair." I was not prepared for a test that affected my child. This test made me aware of my need to trust God with my child. After many tears and lots of struggling, I told God, "She is your child. Your love for her is perfect. You have a perfect plan for her life." I told God that I trusted Him with my daughter, regardless of the outcome.

God has been faithful through my daughter's illness. She has undergone a brain surgery that helps alleviate her symptoms. She takes medication and receives periodic injections that help relieve the pain of the muscle spasms. She handles these difficulties with a smile on her face and joy in her heart. She has a job that makes a difference in the lives of children and families in traumatic situations. She loves God and shares His love with others.

Each of these tests has revealed a need in my life. Through each difficult trial, I have learned something important. Through the death of my son, I learned of God's unconditional love and forgiveness. Through the escape from my abusive marriage, I learned of my need for a relationship with Christ. Through my daughter's illness, I learned to trust Him when circumstances were not to my liking.

Do you find yourself facing a test you are unprepared for? Is the material difficult? Do you need help from someone, or something bigger than yourself, to pass this test?

Jesus is the One who has the answers. He came to Earth, lived among us, and died on the cross to pay the penalty for our mistakes. He rose again so we may live forever with Him. He desires a relationship with you. He wants to walk alongside you and help with all life's tests and trials. All you have to do is ask. Invite Him into your life.

There is no need to wait. Now is a perfect time to begin your relationship with Jesus. Pray with me now:

"Jesus, I know I have made mistakes. I believe You came to Earth and died on the cross to pay my penalty for those mistakes. I believe You were raised from the dead, so I can live forever with You. I choose to have a relationship with You. I invite You into my life. Amen."

Michelle Ruddell is a high school math teacher in Robinson, Texas. Now an empty-nester, she is working on sharing the stories of God's faithfulness through the death of her son, her escape from an abusive marriage, and single-parenting her two daughters. Michelle teaches a single-adult Bible study class and volunteers with "Light in the Gap," a ministry to women just released from prison. Read more at

ReflectionsonBitsofGlass.blogspot.com.
*Contact Michelle on Facebook or at **MRuddell21@gmail.com.***

Thoughts to Ponder
from Are You Ready for the Test?

1. Decisions should never be made before seeking God's wisdom.

2. Even when we are unprepared, God will walk through the test with us.

3. Don't choose a short-term solution for a long-term problem.

> ## **What test are you going through right now?**

Your word is a lamp for my feet, a light on my path. — Psalm 119:105

Are We There Yet?

by Cherry Fargo

If you've ever been on a trip with a child, you are probably familiar with the questions, "Are we there yet?" "Will we be there soon?" and "How much longer until we get there?" Maybe you remember asking those questions when you were young. For some reason, even from an early age, we tend to develop expectations that everything will be better when we arrive at our destination.

I carried this expectation through my life, believing I'd find my true identity in each phase that I entered. At age eighteen, I expected to be fully me, but it wasn't long before I realized, that wasn't going to happen. I pinned my hopes on my twenty-first birthday, with no results. Then I thought marriage would give me some clarity about myself, but it didn't. Finally, I thought being a mom would unveil my identity, but even that privilege fell short of revelation. None of these destinations brought me any closer to feeling like I knew who I was or had finally arrived at the destination of coming into my own and feeling fulfilled.

Why was I so intent upon having my identity defined by something external? Because I grew up with a stepfather who was abusive—physically, sexually, and emotionally. He often told me, "You are so stupid. You'll never amount to anything." I was desperate to prove him wrong. Also, I was determined to rescue my younger sister, his biological daughter, from our haunting past.

She was just six years old when she entered my room and sat on my bed with what seemed like the weight of the world on her shoulders. The eleven years that separated us did nothing to lessen the unjust sense of responsibility that she felt. As grief and remorse spilled out of her mouth, my heart broke in a way most seventeen-year-olds never experience. "I'm sorry for the things my daddy did to you," she said.

I thought, *Wasn't I really the one who had failed her?*

He'd done the same things to her and worse. If I'd only known, maybe I could have protected her. It was a heavy burden to carry.

My stepfather ended up doing time for his unsolicited actions. For seven combined years of abuse, he was sentenced to five years of prison for each one of five criminal charges. However, he served his sentences concurrently, so instead of spending twenty-five years in jail, he only served five. He never confessed, never admitted his guilt, and never repented.

Even though I had professed a belief in Jesus as the Son of God at a young age, these things made me think God had let both my sister and me down. Therefore, I decided I would not acknowledge a god whom I felt had abandoned us. This is where my journey to rely on myself and define my own identity began. With each passing milestone, I felt more and more disappointed.

A few years into my stepfather's sentence, my mother decided that she, my siblings, and my grandmother, would move 3,000 miles away from northern California to Texas. I thought I would come to the Lone Star State for a few years and then return to NorCal. Instead, I met a guy and got married. So here I am. Still here.

Before I became a mother, I had done enough reading and research to understand that abuse is often passed from one generation to the next. The abused is more likely to become an abuser. That was not a legacy I wanted to leave my children. But when I arrived in Texas, just a few years before becoming a mother, I was without friends and community. I worked outside of the town where I lived. Although my mom resided next door, she was busy raising my younger siblings. I confess that I still held some resentment toward her. I felt as if she was partly to blame for the things my sister and I had suffered. Even if she had tried to give me advice, I would not have trusted it.

A few years into living in Texas, I was now a mother with a nine-month-old baby and another on the way. My husband was working full-time and going to school full-time. Without any help or resources, I felt isolated and alone. No effort to find fulfillment had worked, and I was certain of only one thing: I was lost. I didn't know what I was doing or how to find my way. And no one was there to show me. I wanted more for my children than I had growing up. I desired a marriage that wasn't dysfunctional. I longed to feel like my life wasn't a failure. However, I only knew all the things *not* to do and none of the things I *needed* to do to get where I wanted to be. I still wondered when I'd finally arrive.

Even though I had spent a decade walking away from Him, God was always there, gently pursuing me. The only times I ever felt safe as a child were when I went to church or attended various church activities with my biological dad. I decided I had nothing to lose by redirecting my path back toward God. I wanted to live a transformed life, and I was finally willing to change my course to do so. I needed to shed my sin of self-sufficiency, declare that God was my destination, and affirm that Jesus was the only Guide who could lead me to where I needed to be. By saying yes to following Jesus, I found peace, hope, direction, purpose, and even the fulfillment I had been so desperately seeking. I felt as if I had finally arrived.

Following Jesus hasn't always been easy, and it hasn't meant that life was without challenges. But it has always been worth it. God has shown up in every difficulty I faced. He preserved my marriage when it was about to fail. My husband and I are about to celebrate twenty-three years together. Our family life has been far less dysfunctional than it could have been, because we look to Jesus to guide us. God has blessed us with four fabulous children who have never known what it is like to have divorced parents or to experience the debilitating abuse like my sister and I endured. They are healthy and well adjusted, and I am trusting that they will all one day find themselves chasing after God.

In fact, not long ago during a worship and prayer night for the youth mission trip, God gave me a glimpse of His power at work in my children. Adult after adult got up to speak inspiring words over the youth. After a while, my seventeen-year-old daughter rose up and passionately delivered words of encouragement over her peers. I was reminded that my seventeen-year-old self was running away from God as fast as she could, and here my daughter was, running *toward* Him as fast as she could. God's Word speaks about parental baggage being passed down three or four generations. However, He stops the cycle for those who choose to love Him, and he promises to pour out His blessings on a thousand generations. Being on God's path makes a difference, not just in our own lives, but also in the lives of those around us.

My sister took most of her life to find freedom and identity. She tried to bury her pain in drugs, promiscuity, and a string of bad relationships. She struggled with bipolar depression and multiple personality disorder brought on by the abuse she endured as a young child. She had always longed for reconciliation with her father. She hoped that one day he would admit his guilt and apologize. In October of 2015, her father died, and she never received that apology. To add insult to injury, many members of our family said things like, "The world is a better place without him," or, "Good, I hope he rots in Hell."

Once again, my heart broke for her. If anyone in my family had a right to say those things, surely it was me. Instead, I experienced an inexplicable grief, which lingered in my heart for days. I prayed and prayed and finally understood my sorrow. You see, God loves everyone, and His desire was for my stepfather to repent. He would have been forgiven in a moment, because he was God's creation. Not to excuse his behavior or minimize the effects of abuse, but I believe he acted out of his own wounds and brokenness. The truth is, my stepfather is eternally separated from God, from peace, and from healing.

I had the privilege of walking out my faith in front of my sister year after year. Finally, in the spring of 2016, she agreed to a three-day retreat where she finally experienced what it meant to have a loving Father in God. Her life was radically changed by Jesus that weekend, and she came away healed from her multiple personality disorder. She experienced a freedom, a joy, and a peace she had never known before.

The reason I share my sister's story with mine is twofold. First, our faith journeys were impacted by the same events. In May of 2017, I had the opportunity to speak to a women's group about our story, and my sister went with me. The night before, I stayed with her and my mother, and God orchestrated an amazing time of healing for the three of us. After the meeting the next morning, my sister felt a call on her life and expressed her desire to speak hope and encouragement into the lives of others who were abused. She even hoped we could speak together someday.

Second, nine days after our special time together, my sister passed away suddenly and unexpectedly. While I still grieve losing her just before her thirty-sixth birthday, I also rejoice at the thought that she is now in the presence of God, fully healed and made whole, just as He created her to be. I also have joy in knowing that I will see my sister again in Heaven. God has promised that those who turn from doing things their own way and commit to following after His Son Jesus, who died on a cross for our forgiveness and rose again, will have eternal life with Him. I can't think of a better destination.

Do you ever wonder, *When will I get there?* or *How much longer will this take?* If so, consider yielding your "right of way" today. By doing so, you could find yourself exactly where you were always meant to be. If you admit that you have gotten lost trying to go your own way by relying on your own knowledge, then ask Jesus to forgive you of your sin and to guide you on His path, not yours. God will be faithful to give you a new identity and transform your life as you pursue Him. It is as simple as, "Trust in the Lord with all your heart and lean not on your own understanding; in all your ways submit to Him, and he will make your paths straight" (Proverbs 3:5–6).

I am thankful that I have finally arrived. Won't you join me?

Cherry Fargo *and her husband have been married twenty-three years, and together with their four children, call North Texas home. Cherry loves to create faith-based home décor for her business, "Being Remade," as well as write for her blog,* ***TheBeingRemadeLife.com***. *She aspires to write and speak words of hope to encourage, empower, and equip others to embrace being remade in the image of Christ.*

Thoughts to Ponder

from Are We There Yet?

1. Being a child of God is the only identity we need.

2. Childhood wounds can only be healed by God.

3. Stop waiting to "get there," and do something right where you are.

How have you lost your way?

But you are a chosen people, a royal priesthood, a holy nation, God's special possession, that you may declare the praises of him who called you out of darkness into his wonderful light. — 1 Peter 2:9

Loved at Last

by Michelle Welch

Have you ever been bullied? Have you ever felt unloved, abandoned, isolated, and alone? Then you have felt like me.

I was born and raised in Vietnam—the oldest girl of six children. My father was a well-known pilot. My mother had a good job with the United States government. We lived above average in a gated community, with live-in maids and a driver. And with that kind of privilege came an all-girls private school.

From an outside perspective, family life surely must have looked good. However, it was full of chaos. My parents were *absentee* parents. Throughout my childhood, I didn't feel cherished, loved, or nurtured. My parents' frequent fighting brought turmoil and madness to the house, mostly because of my father's many affairs with movie stars, well-known singers, and dancers. As a child, I was raised to show no fear, no emotion, and no weakness. Still, my parents told me again and again that I was tall, skinny, and ugly. I also stuttered, and they faulted me for that too.

Many times while my family went on vacation, I was left at home. I became an outlet for my parents' frustration and anger. I was their punching bag. Nothing I ever did was right or good enough. I had to hide from them, or I got a beating. My father beat and kicked me, then left in disgust, saying it was my fault. Then my momma beat me because I had chased my father away to one of his girlfriends. The more I was beaten, the more rebellious and defiant I became, an outcast within my family. And as an outcast, I became a tough tomboy. I started a boy gang, and I was the leader. We got away with terrorizing the neighbors, because they were too afraid of my father to complain or report our activities to the police.

When I was thirteen, I overheard my mom and aunt talking about how they'd been asked by their cult to use me as a human sacrifice. Fear overwhelmed me, and I cried. I don't know how I moved from where I was standing, because my legs were frozen. However, the next thing I knew, I was wandering around the local market.

All my life, whenever I heard the city church bells ring, a peace fell over me. In that moment of fear, I went inside the church. A man was there, peacefully hanging on a cross. I didn't know who He was, because my family was Buddhist. I told Him, "I don't know who You are or why You have to hang on the cross, but I want to have the peace You have. Help me." At that moment, peace surrounded me, and I fell asleep at His feet. When I woke up, I wandered around for a few days.

When I got hungry, I went home. Knowing that I would get the beating of my life, I made up a lie for my parents. To make an excuse for being gone, I told them I had been kidnapped. Nobody believed me, and I was still beaten. I also became the laughing stock of my family.

However, life was never the same after hearing my mother and aunt discuss making me a sacrifice. I withdrew from my family in fear and distrust, because I didn't know when they would come and take me to kill me.

Who could I tell? The police? No, my family had the police department in their pocket.

In my fear, I became more rebellious and careless. Numb emotionally, I didn't care. I felt like an outsider, not belonging anywhere.

At age fourteen, my cousin came to live with us so he could train for and join the Air Force. Showing pity on me, he gave me hugs when I was beaten. He gave me candy and told me how pretty I was. He was the first person who had ever told me I was pretty. In his drunkenness six months later, he bashed my head, raped me, and left me for dead, then went AWOL. Both my parents were vacationing with my brothers and sisters. My maid was taking care of me. She never told my parents what happened. I didn't either. I was hurt emotionally by the pain and the shame. My body started to shut down. I wanted to die. I didn't eat or drink, wasting away until I weighed only seventy pounds. When I finally got the strength to live again, I had to learn to eat and walk.

As I turned fifteen, just when I was getting better, my entire family and I were airlifted to the United States. They told us we were going on vacation, but actually left Vietnam for good. Because of my father's position and my mom working with the U.S. government, unlike so many others, we received the opportunity to move to America. However, the transition was tough. I didn't read, write, or speak English. I hated the foreigners' language.

In the beginning, the best thing about this move was that my mom and dad seemed to get along better. But the happiness between them lasted only for a couple years. My father continued his affairs, and he eventually left us for a younger woman. My mom then had to work three jobs to support five children. This is where my co-dependence came to the rescue. I became an instant mom to my siblings. While going to school, I worked to help my mom raise the family. Life was tough, but there were no more beatings. My father was gone, and she was too tired to beat me.

Before my father left, my cousins visited from time to time, including the one who had raped me. Mom cooked lavish dinners for them. Since my cousin was a guest in our home, I was supposed to serve him with a smile on my face. I refused to do so, and I locked myself in my room. I was beaten for my behavior, even though I was nearing adulthood. That did not help my anger.

On my eighteenth birthday, I planned to confront my cousin about what he had done, but he killed himself before I had the chance. On his deathbed, he confessed to his sister. Instead of getting some justice for his confession, my cousins were unable to deal with their shame and blamed me for his suicide. For ten years, they kept the confession a secret from everyone.

When I was twenty-one, I wanted to know more about Jesus, so I joined the Carmelite Sisters convent. Life as a sister was peaceful. I spent a lot of time in service and prayer, but something in my spirit told me I wasn't developing a personal relationship with God. After two-and-a-half years, I moved to Austin, Texas. I desired that relationship and asked Him to show me who He was. He led me to a house where there was a prayer meeting. I accepted Jesus into my heart that night. As I left the house, I heard a sound like a freight train. The leaves around me clapped, and the wind swirled and covered me and my car with leaves and flower petals. All nature and God's creatures were celebrating. Colossians 1:27 says that God has chosen to make known the glorious riches, which is Christ in you, the hope of glory.

Not long afterward, I met my future husband, Don. By age twenty-five, I had my first child, Megan. Due to complications, I was told I could not have any more children. Even with that news, her birth was a happy but challenging time. I was also terrified. I didn't know how to be a mother. I did want more children after

Megan, though, and I took fertility treatments. After five years, I went to the Lord in prayer, and I sensed God saying I would have a baby boy. Two years later, that word came true—I had a baby boy *without* the help of any IVF treatments. It was a miracle! God blessed us with Jason.

The most wonderful day of my life became a nightmare. Jason was born with a heart defect. He had five surgeries and spent nine months in hospitals. I loved him, but I didn't want to see him suffer. I asked the Lord to take him, but to let me know the day he was going to go so I could say goodbye. The Lord honored my request and woke me up to say goodbye. My baby boy died of complications from his last surgery. I was with him twenty-four hours a day. I could not leave him to go home.

One month after his death, I broke down crying—ugly crying. I asked God to take me home to be with my son. However, a still small voice asked, "Do you love Jason?"

I said, "Yes," crying louder.

A second time I was asked, "Do you love him?"

Again I said, "Yes," crying even louder.

God could see my love for my son. He asked me once more, "Do you love your son?"

"Yes," I said, "of course."

Then I heard Him ask, "When your son died, did he save anyone?"

"No," I said.

"That's why I sent My Son, so you can see your son again."

This time, I cried louder than ever before. I didn't know how to love like God, who gave the sacrifice of His Son. I asked God to give me the love like He has, and so He did.

Still, Jason's death was tough on my marriage and family. We had a million-and-a-half dollars of hospital bills and no baby. My husband became angry with God and turned toward drugs to escape. Our business, finances, not to mention our marriage, went downhill fast. He became a different person, verbally abusive at first, then emotionally and physically. The joy of having a loving husband and father was gone. I had lost him. Life became a living hell. Not only did I have to deal with all the bill collectors on our home and business, but the emotional and physical abuse was out of control.

After one beating, I had to call the police. But I was the one who was taken to jail, because I refused to tell on my husband. If they took both of us to jail, then my children would have been handed over to Child Protective Services. So I took the Fifth Amendment, and I was taken to jail. To show you how horrible things were as he tried to control me, my husband often reminded me of my stay in jail. "You are not an American citizen," he said. "If you get into more trouble, I'll call federal officials to send you back to Vietnam and take your daughter from you."

Amazingly, three years later, I was pregnant with Kayla. The pregnancy itself was another miracle. All the doctors recommended that I have an abortion because I couldn't carry Kayla full-term. But I did make the full term. By now, Don had gone to rehab and straightened out his life. We were happy. However, a year later, Don went back to drugs. The violence resumed, plus he was having an affair. He even brought the woman to my house.

I was devastated. The fighting, violence, and disgrace never seemed to reach a peak. Whenever Don got angry, beat on my head, and demanded money for his drugs, my ten-year-old took her baby sister and ran out of the house, crying. One day, crying, my little girl asked, "What would happen to us if Daddy killed you? Where would we go?"

Her questions were a wake-up call for me. I immediately promised that we would leave.

In 1997, I packed each of us a bag of clothes and headed to the state park with our camping equipment and food. It was so cold. Every night in the tent, we huddled around the heater to stay warm. Our campsite became our home.

Two months later, someone stole our home. They took our clothes, equipment, food—everything. Our little safe house was gone. Distraught, heartbroken, and desperate, I called my sister in California. She and her husband had two vacation houses in Texas, fully furnished, and I asked permission to use one of them. When I called, she didn't give me an immediate answer. She wanted to discuss it with her husband first. We lived in our car, waiting for word from my sister. And when we finally heard back, the answer was no.

It was the lowest point of my life. The rejection was devastating. If people in my family didn't care for us, who would? Thoughts came for me to end it all, for all of us, down at the lake. No one would miss us. No one cared. But God intervened and reminded me how precious Megan and Kayla were to Him, how they really belonged to Him. I broke down and cried, asking forgiveness. "God is our refuge and our strength, an ever-present help in trouble. Therefore we will not fear" (Psalm 46:1–2).

We continued living in our car and God sustained us. A man with a food truck stopped by the car one day to make a sale. But he was touched by the love of God and stopped by every three or four days. He filled our ice chest with food and gave us milk for Kayla.

While serving in the Kairos Prison Ministry, we met a woman who took us into her one-bedroom apartment and lavished love on my children. I believe God brought this woman to my girls and me, because I decided to give to His children in prison.

We prayed for my husband every day. After about a year, he hit bottom as a drug user and womanizer and went back into rehab. We got back together. We had three years of peace together, good years, and my children had a father.

When Megan was fifteen and Kayla was five, Don was killed by a drunk driver. His death was shocking and painful for all of us.

One month later, in December, we were celebrating Jesus' birthday, and I was talking with Kayla about the birth of Jesus. I was still sitting there with a sad heart, also asking God, "Where is my husband?" But Kayla, who had been going to speech therapy for two years, suddenly spoke to me in a crystal clear voice, "Mom, did Jesus die for me?"

I said, "Yes, honey, He did."

Then Kayla said, "My daddy is in Heaven with my brother Jason."

That's when God asked me directly, "Why do you doubt he is with Me? I never forsook him. He ran from Me, but he was always Mine."

That gave me complete peace. I cried with a thankful heart.

I was left behind, however, to deal with the financial problems from years of Don using drugs and partying. I didn't know if a single mom working two jobs could support two girls and deal with those issues. I shouldn't have worried. God surrounded us with strong Christian friends to stand with us and be mother and father figures to my girls.

Years later, being single and serving the Lord in church, prison, and women's shelters, I prayed for a godly man, not only to be a husband but also to be a father to my children. I wanted a righteous man who loved God and served Him—someone who was humble, with high morals and values, who was kind, sensitive, and generous—someone who would love and protect us. All my friends laughed, saying I would be single for a long time. I was okay with that. I didn't want a man who was not from God.

My God and Father is so good. He blessed me with that man. Someone also named Don. God found him in prison! No, not locked away in a cell. He was also serving in prison ministry. Don was more than what I had asked. God has used him as a conduit for healing and to teach me how to trust again. I am a blessed woman every day, loved by my Father and at last, by my husband, who honors me.

God lovingly taught me to surrender, and I slowly got in touch with my emotions. That released my pain and shame. God restored and strengthened me. I had never felt so free, so loved, and so beautiful. With the support of people who love God, I have connected with people at a deeper level.

My heart leaps with joy and passion to see men and women like me set free. I want to help other women find freedom like I have found—to realize they are loved, just as I am, by the one true God. "Stand firm. Let nothing move you. Always give yourselves fully to the work of the Lord, because you know that your labor in the Lord is not in vain" (1 Corinthians 15:58).

Through my healing, I have found strength and courage to tell my sister, who is a retired police officer, what happened to me and why I ran away from home so many years ago. For thirty-five years, my family had been making fun of the kidnapping story. Once my sister confirmed the story that I had told her, she promised they would never make fun of me again—and she apologized.

I no longer blame or reject myself because of others. I have learned to love myself as God has loved me—to see who I am in His eyes. I am His beautiful creature, His beloved rose, a priestess to the Kingdom. I'm a work in progress, but I know that God is there for me, so I yield myself daily to Him.

I feel free today. I no longer wear a mask. I am forever changed and loved. My Lord continues to work through me.

Are you restless and burdened? Do you feel lonely and worthless? Do you regret the pain in your life or feel like it's too much for you? Are you so hopeless that you don't see your way out? Or are you angry and bitter? I want you to know about my friend the Lord Jesus, my burden carrier, my shelter, my hope, my strength. He is the only Son of God, the one I met in church, the one who hung on that cross for my sin, my rejection, my pain—for my shame and yours. He rose from the dead on the third day and defeated death. So death has no hold on Him. Do you want eternal life without regret, shame, or pain—to walk in the belief of His finished work? Then you can pray this prayer and believe in your heart. "Lord Jesus, thank you for dying for my sin and taking all my pain and shame on the cross. You rose from the dead to give me life through Your precious blood, which has washed me clean of all my sin. Now I am a child of God, and I have eternal life through You."

Satan knows your name but doesn't call you by that. He calls you by your sin. God knows your sin, but He calls you by your name.

Michelle Welch grew up in South Vietnam. Raised in the middle of conflicts, Michelle found peace and strength in an image, a casting in bronze of an unnamed man chastened and tortured as she herself felt. Though the troubles in her life continued to come and go, that man always abided with her, beckoned to her, and became her dearest consultant and confidant. She came to know Him as Savior, King, and Friend. Michelle is active in the Operation Care Homeless Ministry and can be reached at
Servant_4_Jesus@sbcglobal.net.

Thoughts to Ponder
from Loved at Last

1. Supernatural peace is available to anyone.

2. If we listen, God will lead.

3. God gave us His Son, and in turn we need to give Him our children.

Who do you need to give to the Lord?

God is our refuge and strength,
an ever-present help in trouble. — Psalm 46:1

Little Orphan Nanny
by Nancy Kehr

Author Avijeet Das once said, "You may keep wandering in life all the time, but one day life will take you to the place where you are meant to be!" During my childhood, my sister, two brothers, and I were wanderers, because we trekked from home to home, scattered throughout California and Nebraska, where various relatives and strangers reluctantly took us in.

Our parents were unable to care or nurture us on a regular basis. My mother's neurological illness waxed and waned, and my father often worked more than one job to keep up with over-burdening medical costs. I felt neglected, and my life was disjointed. I don't have a lot of fond memories of family, traditions, or feelings of belonging. Memories of good times are few.

Even with other family members helping us out, the task of caring for three younger children fell to me. Although there wasn't much difference in our ages, the two youngest treated me like their mother.

A few positive memories peek through the curtain of my soul every now and then. God, church, the Bible, and songs had all been introduced to me, and there were times when church attendance was regular. Those good times built up my heart for the unpleasant times. I loved being at church. It felt like "home."

For the most part, however, I was not raised as a Christian. Our family's circumstances and a lack of extended family support left us more isolated than not. I guess you could say I felt like "Little Orphan Nanny" waiting for "Daddy More-Bucks" to save me. With cardboard in my shoes and no coat or sweater to protect me from the cold, my ability to hope and trust was hindered. Hindsight revealed Satan's plot to keep me from a true, fatherly relationship with my Creator.

God's ability to protect and direct all of us throughout our young lives amazes me. A certain drive to please God burned deep within my gut. Nearly as strong was the desire to stay in school.

At age thirteen, my father left our home, taking my two younger brothers with him. My sister ran away, leaving me to care for a very disconnected, disabled mother. Because of this, I didn't know if I would have a home, school, or anyone to watch over me. Just when I didn't know how I was going to continue by myself, my mother asked a family at church to temporarily care for me. I ended up living with them for the better part of my teen years, and I believe God placed this surrogate family in my life for a good reason. Being around the father of this family helped me see the qualities of a real man and a caring father. I am forever grateful to Daddy-Bob Moon for his steadiness, his love for his family, his work ethic, his banjo music, his faithfulness to God, and so much more. My heart took it all in.

Because of the effect my "adopted" dad had on me in my early adult years, my goals for the future were even more cemented. I wanted my own children to have a solid spiritual foundation, and I painstakingly searched God's promises and spiritual principles for myself. For me, an important spiritual principle was more easily remembered if I put it into a song. As a result, I wrote many songs for my kids, but the songs helped me too.

Discovering that God was a Father to the fatherless, I gave myself permission to allow my heavenly Father to be the substitute for all that hadn't been right for me as a child. Little by little, our relationship grew until I became closer to Him and more confident. Out of that confidence, I penned the words to this little ditty. I have shared the lyrics before, but I have never shared the reason it came into existence. I call it my nyah-nyah-on-the-devil song. Imagine it being sung in the voice of a smug, little girl, skipping as she sings.

I Am His Little I Am

I am my Father's glory,
I am His joy and pride!
I barge right into the Throne Room,
I run right up to His side!
I try to be just like Him
In all I do or say.
I'm spoiled, and I know it,
But He loves me anyway!
Oh . . . I am His little "I am." I am!
Runnin' around the Throne.
In the name of my Big Brother, Jesus,

130

I make all Heaven my home.
I am His little "I am." I am!
Some say I look just like Him.
I am His little "I am." I am!
I am, 'cause He lives within.
Oh, I am, 'cause He lives within!
Happy Father's Day, Father God.
Happy Father's Day to my Daddy-Bob.

Thank you both, because I don't have to wander anymore. I love you dearly.

Nancy Kehr *has combined the power of the Word and the power of the pen for inspiration and instruction. Many of her stories, poems, or songs are found at* **SongsatNight.wordpress.com**. *As a Dental Practice Consultant, and later the Owner/Director of a Dental Assisting School, Nancy seized frequent opportunities to enter people's lives to share Jesus. She delights in mentoring young women and ministering to the homeless. Her line of greeting cards,* FaithLines by Nancy, *will be available soon.*

Thoughts to Ponder
from Little Orphan Nanny

1. The best father you can have is your heavenly Father.

2. No matter what your beginnings were, you can finish strong in Christ.

3. God knows your destination.

How has God shown His father-like qualities to you?

A father to the fatherless, a defender of widows, is God in his holy dwelling. — Psalm 68:5

Drugs, Sex, and Rock 'n' Roll
by Debra Nussbaum

It started out so promising. Debbie was adopted as an infant by a Jewish couple. However, six-year-old Debbie began to lie and steal money from her mother to buy candy. Thinking that was odd behavior for someone so young, her mother took her to a child psychiatrist. Debbie was placed into a psychiatric ward at UCLA for observation and testing. One test entailed putting electrodes on Debbie's head and back, which was terrifying for such a young girl.

In the psychiatric ward, Debbie befriended an older girl who became a confidante and protector. Debbie's parents came to visit just once a week, and when it was time for them to leave, Debbie cried. "Please, Mommy, don't go!" She ran as fast as she could, chasing them down the hallway.

"You'll be all right. We'll be back next week." When they walked away, Debbie pounded on the door, tears streaming down her face.

When her parents were gone, the attendant forced Debbie into a small concrete room with only a door. She stayed there for hours, alone and isolated. Sitting on the floor, holding her knees and crying, she rocked back and forth. When the attendants weren't around, the older girl talked to Debbie through the door and calmed her down.

Her parents didn't realize that their daughter was being placed in isolation for punishment of even a *minor* infraction of the rules. Once she was placed there because she fell asleep on the floor under the older girl's bed. Debbie didn't feel safe in her own room. She was in the ward for seven months.

When she went back home, her parents divorced. Her mother suffered from panic attacks, smoked pot, and didn't leave home often—except to see a therapist. When Debbie went to elementary school, her mother went back to work and hired a babysitter, Carmen, for after-school care.

When Debbie was twelve, Carmen let Debbie drink alcohol and smoke pot. She taught her how to have sex with boys. One time, she brought Debbie to her apartment along with a young boy and an older man. "Come on," she said. "Take off your clothes and climb into bed."

With all four of them in bed, Carmen explained to Debbie and the boy what to do, step-by-step. Debbie decided she liked drinking and smoking pot and cigarettes. She enjoyed having sex more than she enjoyed school. She started to skip classes, and after a while wasn't going to school at all. Instead, she and this boy hung out, drinking and smoking.

At a family dinner, her mother said, "Your brother said you've been smoking. Is that true?"

Debbie just shrugged.

"I'll tell you what. If you can light up a cigarette right now in front of me and show me that you know how to puff it, I'll let you smoke." She handed Debbie a cigarette. Debbie puffed away as she had been doing secretly for a long time. From that time on, her mother sent her to the store to pick up cigarettes and let her buy a pack for herself at the same time.

When the school notified Debbie's mother that her daughter had been skipping school, her mother couldn't deal with it, so she sent her to Northridge Psychiatric Hospital for Adolescents, where she was given prescription drugs to control her behavior. After six months, her behavior hadn't improved, so they sent her back for another year. During this time, Debbie thought, *There must really be something wrong with me. My mother doesn't think I'm normal, so I must be bad. Am I going to have to live in a psych ward most of my life?*

The only thing that numbed her feelings was drugs.

When she was fifteen, she came home again and resumed the same behavior as before. A truant officer showed up at the house and said, "Do you realize your daughter hasn't gone to school this whole year, except for two days?"

"What?" Frustrated and in shock, she called Debbie's father and asked if he would let Debbie stay with him. "I can't handle her," she told him. "She's out of control."

Staying with her father, she transferred to a different school. Again, she skipped classes.

When her dad found out a few months later, he confronted her. "I heard you haven't been going to classes at school."

"So what? It's no big deal," Debbie said. "School is boring." She turned her back to him.

He came up behind her and slapped the back of her head. "That's your answer?" He lost his temper and started hitting and slapping her. "Don't you see what you're doing? What is wrong with you?"

"I don't know," she cried out. "You put me in psych wards most of my life. You tell me what's wrong." Tears blinded her eyes.

She was then enrolled in the Palmer Drug Abuse Program. When she got out, she went back to her mother's house. Nothing had changed. Her life was about drugs, sex, and rock 'n' roll.

When she turned seventeen, she was again placed in the psychiatric ward.

"So what are you going to do this time?" Debbie said to a counselor. "Put me in the cement isolation room when I'm bad?"

"We don't have an isolation room," the counselor said. "Why would you say that?"

"Because that's where I was put for hours at a time when I was a kid."

After arguing back and forth for a few minutes, Debbie said, "Bring me up there, and I'll show you."

They did, and she went over to the bookcase that she remembered. "It's behind here."

They moved the bookcase and discovered that she was telling the truth. A small cement cubicle was within the wall. "We had no idea," the counselor said.

"That's where they shoved me every time I cried when my mother left. They left me in there for hours."

The doctor decided to put Debbie under hypnosis, where information could be revealed about the cement cubicle and other things that had happened. They asked how she felt.

"I'm seventeen and have spent half my life in psychiatric wards. How should I feel?"

"What have you learned through all of this?"

"That I like to party and have sex and use drugs to numb the pain from knowing that no one really cares," she said defiantly.

When Debbie phoned, her mother said, "Well, you're not coming home. I can't handle you anymore."

Debbie hit the streets of Hollywood. Soon she had new friends. She partied with the bands, movie stars, and a few mobsters. She stayed in motels with stoners and liked the fast-paced drug, sex, and party life with celebrities. She was eighteen but told them she was twenty-one. Needing money to support her increasing drug habit,

135

she did what she loved. She danced, working as a stripper on Sunset Boulevard.

Her mother remarried, and Debbie decided to drive back from a Hollywood party to see her. Debbie had been drinking, was high on Quaaludes, and lost control of the car, crashing into a tree. No one stopped, so when the haze cleared from her mind, she somehow managed to drive on to her mother's. She went right to bed.

When her mother saw her in the morning, she asked, "What happened to you?"

Debbie sat up in bed and saw dried blood all over her. "I don't know—I had a dream that I crashed the car, and nobody pulled over to help me." She was confused.

"By the looks of you, that wasn't a dream. Where's the car?"

"I don't know."

They went to the driveway and saw the car—a total wreck.

After seeing the car, the police said to Debbie, "You're lucky to be alive." The car engine is literally in the middle of the car."

Debbie stared at them. "It is?"

"How in the world did you manage to drive it home?"

"I have no idea," Debbie said. "Someone up there must be looking out for me."

Debbie continued to work as a stripper and started working as a high-priced call girl. She went from popping pills and smoking pot to shooting heroin and freebasing cocaine. She attended big Hollywood parties and hung out with rock stars, musicians, and movie stars. She performed in some B movies and even represented "Strippers of America" on the Wally George program in Anaheim. She was proud of these accomplishments and so was her mother, especially when Debbie went to the Playboy Mansion. Her mother kept lingerie and nude photos of Debbie in her wallet and showed them to others with great pride.

As her addiction grew worse, Debbie woke up in motels with people she didn't know.

At the Ritz Carlton, Debbie took a big hit of cocaine and had a grand mall seizure. When she woke up in the hospital, her mother was there.

Her mother explained that someone from the hospital found her on a bench out front and brought her inside. The next morning Debbie pulled her IVs out and escaped.

136

Not long afterward, she was partying at a hotel and doing rock cocaine when she felt a knife at her throat. She was forced into the bathroom, along with another girl, and heard a rough voice say, "Take your clothes off."

Four black men took turns raping the girls.

Debbie couldn't control the spasmodic fear trembling within her. *Are they going to kill us?*

When they were finished, one of the men said, "You'd better not say anything about this."

Not able to speak, Debbie shook her head.

"When I give you the signal," he said, "you'd better run." He pointed his finger in her face. "You keep your mouth shut, or else." He held up his knife.

Debbie nodded.

He swung open the door, and the girls scooped up their clothes from the floor, dashed out of the room, and out of the hotel, running naked down the street of Santa Monica Blvd. They didn't look back, afraid the men might be following.

Debbie hooked up with Phillip, a musician, and got pregnant. Things didn't work out, and she told him to leave. When it was time for the baby to be born, Debbie had to give birth by C-section. Her mother came to the hospital. Debbie had an allergic reaction to the morphine, and the pain kept her screaming and passing out. She delivered a 6 lb. 8 oz. baby boy named Kyle. The doctor prescribed Valium for her, and they placed the baby in intensive care.

"You are the love of my life," Debbie whispered to Kyle. "I'm going to take care of you."

She made a decision to stop selling drugs, but she still used. She got a job as a bartender. For the next few years, Kyle was sick and had kidney problems. Much of Debbie's time with him was at the hospital. They experimented with different drugs and finally said that he would eventually lose his kidney.

"No! There must be something that can be done." Debbie panicked. She called medical facilities and specialists all over the United States, looking for help. Then she discovered that the UCLA hospital had another protocol they could try. She made an appointment, but when she and Kyle arrived, two personnel from the Department of Children and Family Services (DCF) were waiting in the lobby and took Kyle away from her.

"What are you doing?" she screamed. "Give me back my baby!" An officer held her back. "What's going on?" Debbie yelled, her eyes wild with fear. "Where are you taking him?"

She asked her attorney, "What is this all about? How could this happen? Were the doctors here behind this? Why?"

After some checking, he told her, "Actually, it's your mother who is behind this. She said you're still using drugs, and you're not fit to take care of Kyle."

Her mother had been taping Debbie's conversations for several months. She recorded Debbie's complaints about the doctors, her threats to take them to court because they couldn't diagnose and treat Kyle properly, and her angry rants.

"You're in a catch 22," the attorney said. "If you fight your mother, the court will place Kyle in MacLaren Hall during a long investigation and court battle until they determine who is best fit to take care of Kyle."

"And with my background, I know where that could go. MacLaren Juvenile Hall is for abused, unwanted, or neglected children. He's five years old. I don't want him there. I don't want him to go through what I did as a child, living in an institution."

"He's going to need dialysis, and because of your mother's nursing training, she said she could handle that at her home. The judge is going to look at that as a positive."

Debbie gave in, and her mother was awarded custody of Kyle. He was on dialysis for several years and received a kidney transplant when he was eight years old.

Debbie stole several prescription pads from the doctor whom she thought had conspired to take Kyle away from her. Because his name and license number were on them, she simply wrote her own prescription when she wanted drugs. A van she was riding in was searched by the police. They found the forged prescriptions and arrested her. She was threatened with one year for each script, and there were a lot of them. The alternative was to plead guilty to the felony, have one year in jail at Twin Towers in Los Angeles, and go to a six-month rehabilitation drug program.

It was Christmas. She was in jail and had lost everything. An inmate was humming the Christmas carol, *Silent Night, Holy Night*. She looked around her cell. *There's nothing holy about this place.* She felt

138

empty inside. *I wish I had something to fill this void. Some meth would help.* She couldn't sleep. She felt alone and abandoned. *Nobody really cares about me. My mother doesn't want me around. She's probably glad I'm in jail, once again in an institution.*

The next day, her cellmate greeted her. "Hey, bunky, are you a Christian?"

Surprised by the question, Debbie said, "No, I'm Jewish."

"Well, I'm going to teach you how to be a Christian. Teach you how to pray." She handed her a Bible. "Here, start reading the book of John. You'll find out that God loves you." She smiled. "You're going to do a bunch of stuff with me, like come to church and Bible study."

"Oookay," Debbie said. *What is with her?*

Every Tuesday night, she went to a Bible study led by Sandra Evans and Pastor Mark of Prison Ministry of America. She listened to the testimony of Laura and Cocoa, about their former drug addictions and life choices that brought them to prison.

I can relate to that.

"Then everything changed," Laura said, "when I opened my heart to God and accepted Jesus. God loves you and wants to turn your life around, give you hope and a future."

How can that be?

"Read the Bible with an open mind and heart, and let God speak to you. Jesus loves you and has a plan for your life."

Wow, I feel like she's talking directly to me.

Debbie identified with Laura's story and read in earnest, searching to find what these girls had. The words started to come to life for her. Each week after Bible study, she went back to her cell and thought about what was shared.

I've done fourteen years of methamphetamines. At times I've seen demons, shadowy people lurking in corners. I thought I'd be addicted for the rest of my life, so I've learned to deal with it. But the drugs sucked me into the darkness and surrounded me. Drugs are straight from the pit of Hell. My life has fallen apart.

Debbie heard a voice in her head say, *Are you done?*

Tears rolled down her face. "Yes, I'm done. I don't want to run anymore. I don't want to do the drugs. I'm done playing the game. I'm done hurting my son. I'm done hurting my family."

Good, now go in the direction that I ask you to go.

139

She sat in her cell, overwhelmed with the sense that God had just spoken to her. She thought about what Laura had quoted from the Bible—about the promise of having a future and a hope.

I'm going to do an amazing thing. That inner voice again. *Go to the House of Esther.*

She knew that Laura and Cocoa had gone there, and the program had helped change their lives, but she wondered if that was for her. She was facing a felony conviction with a six-month rehabilitation program and three years' probation. Going to the House of Esther for nine months would require her to petition the court for a longer sentence.

Am I losing my mind? Is this really God's voice?

If you want Me to bless you, go in the direction I'm leading you. You have to leave everything you knew behind. Trust Me, and go where I've asked you to go.

"Okay, Lord, I'm willing. I want to change."

The next day, she requested an acceptance letter from the House of Esther to present to the court. She had an overwhelming peace with her decision. The court agreed to sentence her there to complete the nine-month program. She now had a felony conviction with three years of formal probation. After a year, there would be a required progress report.

The next day, someone from the House of Esther picked her up from jail. Scared for the first few weeks, she realized this was going to be different from anything she'd ever experienced. She also knew that she had surrendered and intended to follow through with this commitment to the program—and to the Lord.

When she learned the strict routine she was expected to follow at the house, she lay on her bed that night and cried. *What am I doing here? This is crazy. I can't do this. I could use a shot of meth right now.*

That inner voice of the Holy Spirit spoke. *When you seek Me more than you sought drugs, I will bring you joy and peace.*

From that moment on, she couldn't get enough of His Word. Change started to penetrate her heart through reading the scriptures. Every word seemed to be for her.

One morning she read, *I will never leave you or forsake you.* Next she read Jeremiah 29:11: "For I know the plans I have for you," declares the Lord, "plans to prosper you and not to harm you, plans to give you hope and a future."

Again she heard that inner voice speak. *Give Me all of you, turn your will over to Me, and I will bless you and protect you. I will always be there and will never leave you or forsake you.*

Having felt abandoned and unwanted in her childhood, these words brought comfort and peace.

Even when conflict came up with others in the house, she couldn't get enough reading of the Word, attending Bible studies, and praying. She'd go to her room and seek God. At one point, she and another girl rubbed each other the wrong way. They were instructed to pray together twice a day to resolve the conflict. Through those times together, they bonded and built a close relationship. Day by day, Debbie experienced the power of God's Word to bring change. She learned what real love was, unconditional love—*agape* love.

Debbie was invited to promote Calvary Chapel's Fourth of July Freedom Celebration. She rode a pink House of Esther beach bicycle and passed out flyers and posters. Joy filled her heart as she talked to people and invited them to the celebration, knowing they would hear about Jesus. *I feel like a little kid, full of joy and excited about God.*

When she saw some of the people she had invited actually show up at the event, and she had the blessing of praying with them to accept the Lord, she knew she had a purpose for her life.

When Debbie's graduation day arrived, her mother and her son, Kyle, came. Her graduation from the House of Esther was the first thing she had ever completed in her life. She had stuck it out, made changes, and was grateful for God's goodness.

Her mother stood and shared: "I'm amazed at what happens in the house. Even though I see it and I know it's true, I can hardly believe the change I see."

Debbie's first job after graduation was working at Calvary Chapel Downey as a receptionist. She loved being part of the ministry. She followed Pastor Mark's suggestion to apply for early termination of probation.

Again, she heard God's voice. *I'm going to send you out, even to other nations to proclaim what I've done in your life.*

She wondered how that could possibly happen. *I don't even have a passport.*

You just trust Me and watch what's going to happen.

When her day in court came, Debbie sat with Pastor Mark and one of the girls from the House of Esther. She stood when the judge called her name.

"I see you're two years into your probation, and you've completed everything needed. We have many letters of recommendation through the House of Esther, requesting early release of probation."

The prosecutor made objections to the early release.

"I hear you," he said to the prosecutor, then turned to Debbie. "It's rare to see proof of how someone has turned her life around as you have. We're not only going to go for early termination, we're going to take all the felony charges and drop each of them to a misdemeanor."

Debbie's mouth dropped open in surprise.

Then came that still small voice. *See, My promises are true.*

Debbie looked back on her life and thought, *I remember prostituting myself, drinking, partying, and being high on drugs. Satan likes to sugarcoat his story. Hollywood makes the street life look like you'll live in a fairy tale life. Instead, you get broken dreams, heartache, a life full of emptiness, and no hope. Jesus' story is totally different. He kept me alive, because He had a plan for me. He was waiting for me to answer His call.*

Debra Nussbaum has worked for the past seven years as the Ministry Coordinator for Sound Doctrine Radio Ministry, podcasting, filling orders, working with the web, and bookkeeping. She's traveled to speak in prisons for Bill Glass's "Behind the Walls" ministry in Germany, Africa, Guatemala, and throughout the United States. Debbie became a licensed chaplain. Her passion is to go into jails and share the love of Jesus that changed her life.

Thoughts to Ponder

from Drugs, Sex, and Rock 'n' Roll

1. There is no sin too great for God to forgive.

2. God can heal us from a horrific past.

3. Because of a merciful God, we don't always receive the punishment we deserve.

What has God saved you from?

And so I tell you, every kind of sin and slander can be forgiven. — Matthew 12:31

Flying High
by Wanda Martinez Fuster

You want to fly? Let's go. Let's fly high!

I am a pilot, and I enjoy flying because I am a person who loves challenges, whether in my studies, work, family, business, ministry, or sports. Being an athlete helped prepare my mind, soul, and spirit to fight through problems, and prevail.

Flying has given me the tools necessary for those unexpected life occurrences. In the flying world, steep places can be dangerous. You must pay attention to wind speed and topography. In life, we also have to be aware. Whether in our relationships with friends or our marriages, unexpected things happen—similar to flying.

For me, moving from Puerto Rico to the mainland was like climbing from a 1,000-foot altitude to 5,000 feet. My husband and I came to the United States to plant a church. Our ministry started almost ten years ago with a small Hispanic church in Texas.

The church family had many needs such as food and money to pay rent. Our ministry was climbing slowly, but strongly. We flew steady and without fear, and our ministry foundation was based on the Lord's Word. However, we were flying lean. We didn't have a lot of whistles and bells at the church. We weren't able to sustain a large worship band. We had a few people playing the guitar. Because we were small, we'd often lose our musicians to larger congregations. But we opened and helped the community. One initiative was assisting Mexican students by teaching free GED courses, part of a strong partnership with Christian Community Action of Lewisville, Texas.

After the church was up and running, I tackled another challenge. I was asked by a Spanish television station to be an economics expert on their live newscasts. For many years, I did all this for free. Although the television station did not pay me, I was excited to participate and help the community with my expertise in economics and finance. While doing this job, I was approached by another station, a local affiliate from a different Spanish network, where I would do the same type of on-air analysis. For free again.

However, there was a strange turn of events while working at this station. I believe some of the employees, fueled by jealousy,

144

were trying to harm my reputation by making fun of our ministry using "fake news" based on an allegation by a couple we were trying to help. The couple claimed I was doing something illegal, when our ministry was only helping people fill out different kinds of paperwork, all on the up and up. The station trusted this couples' word over mine, even after I had worked there faithfully for many years.

Unfortunately, the allegations ended my television career, and this situation dragged on in the courts for five years. When one door closes, God always opens another. I started law school, and my husband and I taught chaplaincy classes as well as theology. We graduated hundreds of students over many years. Some of them still serve other ministries, hospitals, and nursing homes. After large amounts of persecution and pressure, God offered us hope and assured us that He was with us.

Exodus 19:4 is meaningful to me. "You yourselves have seen what I did in Egypt, and how I carried you on eagles' wings and brought you to myself." That was a perfect verse for a woman who likes to soar. God takes us into His arms and allows us to "fly over" the enemy attacks.

Allow me to use a few more aeronautical terms. The "angle of attack" is the angle at which the relative airflow meets the wing. This is what determines when a wing will stall. It's important to understand relative wind—the way the air flows over the wing. When this is disrupted, air can no longer flow the way it's designed to go over the wing and lift decreases. Sometimes the lift decreases in our personal lives as well, and many difficult threats affect us.

I was flying my life with a lack of relative wind. My wings were experiencing a lift decrease. Why? Because the enemy of my soul used people to try to stall my flight. I was created to fly freely and openly. However, the Lord gave me another verse for comfort: "[He] satisfies your desires with good things, so that your youth is renewed like the eagle's" (Psalm 103:5).

In our flight of life, we travel to different altitudes, but we always have to descend. For almost five years, I was chased in the courts by a pair of aliens from Mexico. They were deflecting their own sin by accusing our ministry of something wrong. They went public with their false claims at the television station. When we descend, we stabilize and make the final descent to arrive safely.

The Lord was with us the whole voyage, and we descended from the turbulence. We were covered by God's grace and protection.

Serving the Lord over the past decade has been exciting but also difficult after being betrayed by that couple. I worried that when I helped someone, I could be trapped for various reasons. Maybe they wouldn't like my achievements or my personality—or maybe they'd find something else they didn't like. I later realized this kind of fear was not of God. When I decided to confront the people who accused my husband and me, they were aggressive and seemed wicked. They tried to appear as victims and were thinking that their lies would never come full circle, back into their own faces.

The fallout from the situation was devastating. I lost a job, I was ridiculed by a TV reporter, and our ministry went through a difficult time. The storm hit us hard. But there was hope after the storm, when the sun came out to shine.

We all learn how to live without fear, how to believe in the Lord's protection, and how to depend on Him to direct our paths. The Lord promises this during a storm: "[The glory] will be a shelter and a shade from the heat of the day, and a refuge and hiding place from the storm and rain" (Isaiah 4:6).

The air in which the aircraft flies can move in three directions. We shouldn't only consider velocities along the aircraft's flight path. We must be aware of crosswinds, which occur perpendicular to the flight path but parallel to the ground. We must also be aware of updrafts and downdrafts, which occur perpendicular to the ground. From the aircraft, we cannot directly measure the wind speed but must compute the speed of the wind from the ground speed and airspeed. Wind speed is the vector difference between the airspeed and the ground speed.

To translate this into our ministry and life, we were flying high and faster, but we were not able to recognize the wind speed that was affecting our performance, pushing back our flight. After the accusations came against us, we were flying on a pure velocity of our Lord's command.

Eventually, we had a perfect landing, and we praised the Captain of our flight, God, when the judge ruled on a settlement in our favor. The Lord's command was perfect, and our flight path ended up beautiful, because His hand was navigating us. The Lord's biblical promise that He will free us from the enemy became real and powerful in our situation. Psalm 146:7 says, "He upholds the cause of the oppressed and gives food to the hungry. The Lord sets prisoners free."

We cannot be afraid to take on new challenges and adventures, even when we have setbacks or when people betray us. The beauty of life comes from the unique opportunities that arise from the will of God. If we believe God is in charge of the flight plan for our lives, we will be able to fly high over the trouble.

"But those who hope in the Lord will renew their strength. They will soar on wings like eagles; they will run and not grow weary, they will walk and not be faint" (Isaiah 40:31).

Wanda Martinez Fuster is a Professor of Economics at the college and university level and has been an expert and TV personality for economic subjects at Univision and Telemundo, two TV channels in Texas. She flies airplanes and is the Aerospace Education Officer for the Civil Air Patrol on a squadron in North Texas. Wanda is a pastor's wife and has taught Theology and Economics for pastors and ministers for many years at the Universidad de Mayordomia y Liderazgo. Contact Wanda at
ProfessorWandaFuster@gmail.com.

Thoughts to Ponder
from Flying High

1. God helps us to "fly over" problems.

2. With God as your pilot, you will not need a copilot.

3. Despite setbacks, we should still take on new challenges.

What turbulence have you felt in your life?

Have mercy on me, my God, have mercy on me, for in you I take refuge. I will take refuge in the shadow of your wings until the disaster has passed. — Psalm 57:1

Playing Hide-and-Seek with God
by Melissa Fairchild

I was shopping with the most beautiful girl in the world. She had gorgeous red curls and bright, happy green eyes. We were at a major department store looking for a size 3T Easter dress—with extra frills, ruffle-butt tights, and those fold-down socks with the lace, which looked beautiful in patent leather Mary Janes.

She kept running off—admiring tiny purses and teddy bears. She wanted to play hide-and-seek. Afraid I would lose her, I did what any good mom would do to teach an object lesson. I let her get lost.

This was the perfect moment. No one else was in this section. I got quiet and let her wander from rack to rack. Books. Toys. Purses.

I didn't let her see me. I kept hiding until I watched panic slowly set in—all over her little body. Her eyes got wide. Her feet started running. Her eyes darted all around, looking for safety. Her little voice called out: "Mommy. Mommy? Mommy!"

I let that go on for about thirty seconds before I scooped her up in my arms. "It's okay, baby doll. You're safe. Mommy's gotcha."

She looked up at me with her big green eyes. "I lost you, Mommy. I thought you were gone."

She hadn't lost me. She only thought she had. I was right there all the time.

Have you ever felt this level of panic? I have.

I was seven the first time I felt something like this. My two half-brothers and half-sister were playing behind our apartment building, and I wasn't allowed to play. They had formed a no-Melissas-allowed club. They said they all had something in common—they all knew their biological fathers. I did not.

Mine left before I was born. The only dad I ever knew adopted me when he married my mom—and I'm so grateful. He taught me about God. And by the way he loved me, he showed how much God loves me. I always felt like he was my real father.

Thinking my siblings weren't serious, I ran around the building to play anyway. They circled up. I couldn't believe it. Panic set in as I realized that I was alone, left out. Big tears formed in the depths of my universe. Something shattered. My parents figured out what was going on and formed a let's-walk-to-7-11-to-get-a-Slurpee club that my siblings weren't invited to. From this, I learned to run to my authority figures for comfort. This was the beginning of my trusting God and not people. I felt left out by my siblings, but I felt at peace with God. No matter how dark life got, I never second-guessed that God was for me. I was always welcome in His club.

The next time I felt like this was in high school. At age sixteen, a boy I liked took an interest in me. I was over-the-moon excited. I had his initials, plus my initials, written all over my school notebooks. One afternoon, when I was home alone after school, he came to my house. I was so excited that I ignored the rule about not having friends over when my parents were gone. I let him in, only to find out that he had come with five grown men. They made me go to my room and would not let me out. One by one they came in and took turns doing awful things to me. The boy who I thought liked me left me humiliated, ashamed, and feeling very alone. They warned me that they would hurt my family if I told.

I never told. Not anyone.

In the middle of the whole thing, one of the guys told me he loved me. This shattered my heart. If that was love—and love was what I was so desperately longing for—I didn't really want to be loved anymore. I wasn't sure I even wanted to *live* anymore. It was at this point when I attempted to take my life.

I looked around, couldn't find anyone there to rescue me, and panicked. The shame, embarrassment, and guilt led me to keep this a secret—even from God. Through counseling years later, I was able to open this horrible memory and see that God was there in the room with me that day. He was screaming at those men, "Stop! This is my daughter. You shouldn't be doing this."

But His voice was drowned out by the voices of lust, desire, control, and greed simultaneously screaming, "Do what you want. Take what you want. She's there for you to use."

God showed me that He was there that night to comfort me. He was my pink teddy bear and the blanket I slept with over my head. He was there then and also on so many other nights when I cried myself to sleep and felt alone in my shame. I didn't lose Him—He was right there all along.

These incidents, plus the fact that my bio-dad left before I was born, caused me to have a decades-long thought pattern that said, *You're not good enough. You're not worthy of real love. You're just an afterthought, a second choice. You're not wanted. Get lost! No one wants you around here anyway. If you want love, you'll have to do something to earn it.*

Lies. All lies.

In my senior year in high school, I met the man I would marry. We had a fairy-tale wedding a year later and had two beautiful redheaded, green-eyed daughters.

One day my husband came home and acted strangely. We'd had a great first seven years. We had our moments, but nothing major. I noticed that he had become violent with his words and sometimes with his hands. I confronted him, and he said he did not love me anymore. His hidden porn habit had turned into real affairs over the last three years of our marriage—resulting in his latest girlfriend becoming pregnant. This came without warning. I didn't have any idea this was happening. I guess I didn't want to know.

"Devastated" doesn't begin to describe what I was feeling. Some words I had for the next months after that were *numb, lifeless, severely depressed,* and *hopeless.* Once again, the voices that whispered, "You're worthless and unlovable," crept into my thought-space.

I was angry. Angry at my husband for hurting me in this way and not letting me know for three years. Angry at myself for not having seen this coming. And angry at God for knowing this was coming. I was angry at life in general. I had to move out of my home and back in with my parents, while he moved his pregnant girlfriend into my home. It was humiliating.

So how does a youth minister/housewife cope with this kind of tragedy? In my case, I did not cope very well. I became an entirely different person. I began a secret life of binge drinking on weekends when my kids were gone to their father's house. They say bitterness is a poison you give yourself—hoping the other person will suffer. My drinking and lifestyle of masking my pain through any means necessary was a poison. I felt unlovable. I was taking out all my frustrations all right, but all I was doing was hurting myself.

My lowest point was in the middle of the divorce. I was at a party one night at an apartment when everyone went home at once—everyone but me and the guy who lived there. He kept pouring and I kept drinking, but that last drink after everyone left must have had something in it, because the room began to wobble.

I only remember bits and pieces of a torturous, sick rape that must have lasted a couple hours. I was powerless to stop it. I woke up in an upstairs room—alone. I stumbled around, found my keys, and left, still full of liquor, or whatever it was. I honestly think an angel rode in the passenger seat while I drove home that night, because how I got myself and my car home in one piece is a mystery.

I decided that night that I wanted to reconcile with my husband and make things right with my little family again. My kids deserved a *whole* family—and I was hell-bent on making sure they had one—even if it meant I had to do a makeover on my marriage. My husband agreed to think about reconciliation, but he had already told my parents about me going to a party and drinking.

Considering that news, they kicked me out of their house. Because I had no alternative, I could not take my kids with me. I knew they were safe with my folks. I tried to explain to them about the night before and my transformed heart, but it was too late. The decision had been made. I had been furious with what had happened, and now I was furious that my desire to start over had failed. I lived the next two weeks out of my car, in the back room of the store I managed, one night at a laundromat, and at different friends' apartments. After two miserable weeks, I told my dad I was coming home, taking my kids, getting a divorce, and moving into an apartment. I stopped drinking, reconciled with God, and tried to get my life back in order. I know my dad feels regret over his decision to ask me to leave, but I don't. I needed to hit rock bottom.

Three years later, I was back on my feet, studying for my undergrad in English at the local university and raising my two girls. We moved out of the apartment after a year and back in with my folks so that I could focus on my studies.

During my time at the university, my middle brother died of cancer. My younger sister decided to leave the family—for good. At this point I longed for Heaven—for home. My brother had come crawling out of a life of drugs and into the lap of Jesus just before the cancer set in. We were close in those last two years, and his death only drew me nearer to God.

Life thus far had been a hide-and-seek game with God—mostly the hiding part. However, what happened in 2007 changed the course of my life.

In July, I was in the middle of my summer session at the university, taking Poetry 101. It was my workshop day. I had printed enough copies of my poem for each member of the class and was expected to distribute them and have everyone critique my words. I was nervous. It was Texas-summer hot outside. I was suddenly overcome with nausea. Breakfast became a memory.

After the grueling ninety-minute poetry workshop where my writing was called mediocre at best, I made my way to the on-campus medical clinic. I felt awful.

I gave blood, endured the necessary pee-in-this-cup moment, laid down on the paper-covered table, and waited. I must have fallen asleep, because the nurse practitioner shook my shoulder.

"Miss Fairchild?"

Yes?

"I figured out what's wrong."

Okay?

"You're pregnant."

I almost fell off the table. My mind raced to an awful night four months earlier. I looked at her calendar and pointed to the date.

Yes—I remember. In another situation, I was in the wrong place at the wrong time. It was just one lonely moment during March Madness. Just one.

I pulled into my driveway fifteen minutes later and spied my mom on the porch swing, reading to my six-year-old, whose auburn pigtails wobbled as she flew into my arms. My eleven-year-old was inside, getting ready for the water-park trip that I'd promised them that afternoon.

"Mommy's home!"

My heart felt sick. How could I explain this to my girls? How in the world was I going to make ends meet with another kiddo on the way?

I sent the kids to their bedroom to finish getting ready for the water park and wept uncontrollably. My parents noticed.

All I could think was that my folks were going to be so disappointed in me—again. They were pastors at a local church. How do you tell your dad, who is also your pastor, that you're unmarried and pregnant?

Between sobs, I finally formed the words. "I'm pregnant." The truth escaped my mouth with finality. I repeated it to myself. *Wow.*

Mom asked several questions all at once, but Dad quieted the room. He looked at me, right into my heart, and slowly and deliberately spoke these words: "You are my daughter, and I love you."

In one sentence, years' worth of feeling less-than, used, abandoned, abused, picked last, unlovable, unforgivable, unworthy, and I just didn't belong, came to a grinding halt.

In that one sentence, I felt God speaking through my father.

God spoke to *my* identity "You are My daughter . . ."

God spoke to *His* identity ". . . and I love you."

I belong to Him and am fully loved, because He *is* love.

My son was born a few months later, the most amazing blessing I've ever received. Most kids say, "Momma," as their first word, but not my son. His first words were, "I love you." This is because that's what you say first when that's what you hear most.

After the time I frantically searched for God, I've had many more adventures and mishaps when I thought, *I lost You, God. I thought You were gone.* He has been so faithful to remind me that I hadn't lost Him. He was there all the time.

Since the day my dad spoke those words, I've had a deep-seated knowing that I'm not alone. And the reason I'm not alone is because God is with me. And because God is with me, He won't let me panic for too long.

Since I've had my son, my life has changed. I finished my Bachelor's Degree in English Literature and then earned my Master's Degree in Professional and Technical Writing. I'm still a single mom. I take the fourteen years' worth of experiences I've had as a single parent and used them to mentor single and newly divorced moms. My daughters are seventeen and twenty-one now. Because of their father's addictions and behavior, they rarely see him. They use their stories to mentor teens who have addicted, abusive, or absent fathers.

My son always has a joke that can pull out the sun on a cloudy day. His disposition and unfettered joy are contagious to everyone.

I love that every member of my little family desires to serve others and bring comfort and encouragement.

I hope you feel God speaking to you through the pages of this book, saying, "You are My daughter (son), and I love you." And I hope your life will change—starting today.

If you're going through any of the things I've gone through, please reach out to me or someone in your church. Many churches are places of refuge for hurting hearts like mine.

And if you don't know the God I've been writing about, let's get you introduced by praying a simple prayer together. Whether it is your first prayer, or the first in a while, this is a great place to start.

Hi, God. My name is _____. I know You know me. You created me. I have hidden from You many times. I have also searched for You in many places and many faces, but today I have found You. Please pick me up, turn me around, and save me from where I was headed. I was headed down the wrong path. I know it is not too late. I believe in Your Son, Jesus Christ. Today, I invite You to take charge of my life. Thank You for rescuing me and calming my fears. I want to walk with You for the rest of my life. Amen.

So that's it. You are assured that you'll go to Heaven to be with God forever. Life won't always be easy, but He promises He will never leave you nor forget where you are. The hide-and-seek game is over. Everyone wins.

He really is a good, good Father. The best way to find Him is to stop hiding and start seeking. Jeremiah 29:12–13 says, "Then you will call on me and come and pray to me, and I will listen to you. You will seek me and find me when you seek me with all your heart."

You prayed. He listened. You found Him. What a wonderful beginning.

Melissa Fairchild is a Senior Technical Writer and has taught classes in the subject at college level. She is also an inspirational writer and a single mom. Reach Melissa at HisFairest@gmail.com.

Thoughts to Ponder
from Playing Hide-and-Seek with God

1. Don't play hide-and-seek with God.

2. Look up before you hit rock bottom.

3. A loving word can change the direction of someone's life.

Where do you go and what do you do when your life falls apart?

His eyes are on the ways of mortals;
He sees their every step. — Job 34:21

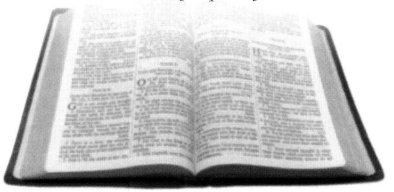

Forgiven, Not Condemned
by Paula Abbott

With an open road before me and a heart wide open, I took off on the journey of my life. This journey ended up becoming my restoration story. As I drove along a country road, I came upon a beautiful old house that had been condemned. After being pounded by all of the elements of life, the outside looked pretty bad. Weeds had grown up around the house. You could hardly see its beauty anymore. I wasn't sure what it looked like on the inside, but if it was anything like the outside, it needed a lot of help, and it wasn't safe for people to be around anymore.

So as my eyes fixated on this house, I saw a sign that said, "Condemned—Do Not Enter. Dangerous." Being curious, I disregarded the sign and walked inside, not sure what I would find. As I stood inside this old house, I could almost hear its cries. It had been abandoned, left alone for years. Lots of places were damaged from overuse—some worse than others. I sensed the laughter that once filled the rooms. The fireplace that sat empty and cold touched my heart. No more warm fires, and no children were giggling as they cuddled up for a long winter's night. I felt so sorry for its emptiness. Then I turned and walked down the hall. There in the doorway were marks with the names of children who had lived in the home, along with their height markers as they grew from toddlers into adults.

Are you still with me on this journey? How many of you remember the marks on the doorway as you grew, year after year? Maybe your children and grandchildren have done this as well.

I felt so sorry for this old house. I felt its loneliness. It once sheltered a family from the storms of life, and now the storms of life had destroyed it. I thought, *This house is me. I was this house.* Once I was full of life, but soon the elements of life tried to destroy me. One by one, everyone rejected me and left me all alone. The things I had done wrong, which the Bible calls *sin* had condemned me to be destroyed. It was like I had a sign hanging on me that said, "Condemned—Do Not Enter. Dangerous." I felt the pain of this house as I remembered my life.

Now, journey back with me to 1961, in a small hospital in El

Paso, Texas. A woman walks in pregnant, ready to give birth to a baby girl. Instead of the excitement of becoming a mother, she has a different plan—which changed the course of her baby's life. That baby was me. My birth mother did not know who my father was, and I was her fourth child. I'm not sure why, perhaps out of shame and embarrassment, but she signed in under another woman's name, and the other woman walked out with me in her arms.

Switched at birth, I began my journey with a mother and father who had struggles of their own. Only six months later, that woman abandoned me and her husband. She put me in my baby bed while he was at work and walked away, never to be seen again. Two months later, he was killed at work.

Alone and broken, I was adopted at the age of eight months.

My adopted father was an atheist, and my mother was a secret follower of Christ. She never shared her faith, because my father would not allow it. We never talked about God, and we never went to church. My father was abusive physically, mentally, and verbally. Do you know what I mean when I say *verbally* abusive? Verbal abuse can leave deep scars that can remain forever.

My adopted family was dysfunctional in every way. Frequent abuse inside my home led to bondage, making me a captive at a young age. At age seven, I was broken and in so much pain, I didn't want to live anymore, so I tried to commit suicide. The abuse continued, and it placed a large void in me. At the age of sixteen, I was desperate for love. I hung out at night clubs, looking for something or someone to fill the void. When you are desperate, you will settle for anything. In my case, I settled for a fast-talking man. I was raped and ended up pregnant. My mother didn't know what to do with me, so she signed me over to my abuser. At the age of sixteen, I was married to my abuser, and domestic violence became part of my life.

Three years of almost daily abuse led to sending my daughter off to another state for adoption. I left my abuser and looked to the world to fill my emptiness. I was never satisfied. I still needed more. So I kept wandering into all the wrong places. In my early twenties, I ended up having two more children by two different men. I was lost, still trying to make a family to fill that void.

Have you ever seen the television show *The Walton's*? I used to watch that show every day. I loved how the family came together

158

and how they really loved one other. I wanted that for myself, so I thought if I could just have children, then they would make me happy.

But it doesn't work that way. People are not designed to make you happy. I later discovered that only God can do that. My children didn't make me happy, and I was still lost and looking.

In my quest for satisfaction, I ended up leaving my two little boys for a life of drugs and alcohol. I moved out-of-state, thinking that everything would get better if I moved. It didn't. For thirteen years, I was a meth addict and an alcoholic. I lost everything—my job, my children, my family, and my home. I was homeless and used whatever I had to purchase drugs. I sold my body and was abused every day by different men. I was lost in a world that could not satisfy my need.

I had never been to church, and I had never heard about Jesus, so I didn't know there was anything better to believe in. Because I was raised in an atheist home, I didn't trust Christian people. I didn't want to become like them. You know, "crazy."

During this thirteen years of out-of-control living, I tried to take my life two more times. On the last suicide attempt, I was placed in a mental hospital. After I was released, I went back to my home state of Texas and struggled for another few years with the drugs and alcohol. But then a miracle happened when I found a Cowboy Church where I heard about Jesus for the first time. Why would someone love me so much to die for me? Then I heard that He was raised from the dead three days later and is alive today, waiting for me to receive His love and ask forgiveness. I would love to say I received Jesus that day, but I didn't. However, a seed was planted in my heart.

Two months later, that truth came alive inside me. I invited Jesus to live in and through me. Due to an overdose of meth, I decided to trust and follow Christ on my deathbed. Because Jesus saved me, today I'm alive to tell my story.

Like the old abandoned house at the beginning of my story, I may have felt condemned, but I was forgiven.

First, I needed to receive the forgiveness of Jesus Christ. Sometimes we ask Him to forgive us, but we never really receive it. So I received His forgiveness, knowing that no matter where I'd been or what I'd done, He still forgave me. The Master Builder of my house came knocking on my door, and all I had to do was open the door and answer His call. He told me that He created me and wanted to buy me back at the highest price, His own life. All I had to do was give Him the deed to my house and trust Him to restore me to His original design. So that's what I did.

Second, I needed to forgive myself. Does anyone struggle with this? I did for years after I received Jesus as my Lord and Savior. I was my worst enemy. I couldn't turn back time, and I wouldn't if I could. God forgave me, and now I needed to forgive myself.

I am who I am today, because of what I have gone through. I can stay in the pit of life, or I can get up and use my story to help others. Praise the Lord! I choose to get up, stand tall, and praise God for all He has given me. I use my story to help thousands of people. Satan wants to keep us in shame, but God wants to set us free. Whatever is hidden in the dark will keep you in bondage, but what comes out in the light will set you free.

Third, I had to ask forgiveness. Remember my three children that I walked away from? They have all forgiven me. I am a wife to an amazing man and a MiMi to some amazing grandchildren. Only Jesus can restore things that were lost. Yes, I have that Walton life now, and I praise God for all He has done.

And last, I had to forgive all of the people who hurt me. Hurting people hurt people. I had to forgive my birth mother for trading me off. I had to forgive the rejection by the people who adopted me. I had to forgive the man who raped me. And I had to forgive my father for all he had done. The forgiveness was for me, not for them. It set me free for the first time in my life.

Jesus loves you so much that He died to give you life. All you have to do is ask Him to forgive you of your sins and come into your heart. Please pray with me.

Dear Lord, I am a sinner in need of a Savior. Jesus, I believe that You are the Son of God and that You died for my sins. Please forgive me and come into my heart. In the name of Jesus I pray. Amen.

Paula Abbott *serves as a co-pastor, evangelist, and inspirational speaker to people in all walks of life. Paula pastors with her husband, Toby Abbott, at Round Pen Cowboy Church, outside of Dallas, Texas. Paula has been in the restoration ministry since 2004. Her story has been featured by CBN's "The*

700 Club." *She has authored three books,* The Good, the Bad and the Ugly, To Experience His Presence, *as well as* Come to the Waters and Thirst No More.

www.RoundPenMinistries.org

Thoughts to Ponder
from Forgiven, Not Condemned

1. Without God, we are condemned.
   With God, we are forgiven.

2. Seeds are often planted in our lives
   before salvation takes root.

3. The hardest one to forgive is yourself.

> ## For what have you not forgiven yourself?

Therefore, my friends, I want you to know that through Jesus the forgiveness of sins is proclaimed to you. — Acts 13:38

The Holy Spirit Broke My Tractor
by Chaplain Ed Yrisarri

Have you ever been aware, either before or after the fact, that you have had an unexpected, perhaps extraordinary, impact from an event? Why did this event occur? Is there something or someone operating in the background or behind the scenes? In other words, is God noticeably and mysteriously working in your life?

Several weeks ago, the steering gears in my tractor failed. I no longer had any steering control. Much to my consternation, I had to stop work and repair the steering mechanism. This required that I dig deep into the assembly to remove and replace the gearing. It necessitated almost complete disassembly and overhaul. After tearing everything down, I realized that I needed to get professional assistance, so I called a tractor mechanic.

Even though I already disassembled and purchased the gearing mechanism parts, the mechanic informed me that there was still one other part required, and it had to be ordered. Another visit would be required to complete the work.

On the second visit a week later, he asked for the missing part. I was surprised. I expected him to arrive with the part in hand. "Oh no," he said. "The part was supposed to be shipped directly to you, and obviously you have not received it. We'll have to wait on the part." Away he went for another week.

Before the next week arrived, I joyfully received the part. When the mechanic arrived for the third time, we were ready to go to work.

The tractor was repaired and reassembled, and I put it to work. But you can imagine my disappointment when suddenly there was a loud blast, and the entire mechanism flew apart. So the tractor mechanic was called back for the fourth time. By now I should have been exasperated, but surprisingly I wasn't. And that was a mystery in itself.

The mechanic quickly identified the problem and went to work. Eventually the repair was complete. Before he departed, I cranked up the tractor and gave it a spin to ensure it held together—and all went well.

In retirement, I work as a volunteer chaplain in the Texas

Tarrant County jails and a few of the state penitentiaries. Each time the mechanic arrived, it was on one of the days I usually work in at least one of the prisons, and of course those days were the only days he could come. Thus, I always requested that he come early so I would have enough time to make my commitments. He was aware of my responsibilities and commitments in the jails. Understanding this, he always accommodated me.

At the end of this fourth repair visit, the mechanic mentioned to me that his stepson was in the county jail, but he did not know his location. I asked for his name so I could find and visit him. He gave me the name, saying he and his stepson had not communicated with each other in quite a long time. The stepson was incarcerated on a capital offense. The mechanic softly asked if I would tell his stepson that he loved him. I acknowledged his request and responded positively. That very day, while at the county jail, I located the young inmate.

Generally, when a pod officer calls out an inmate who has not made a request for a visit with a chaplain, it usually involves bad news.

When the young inmate arrived, and to be sure I was speaking to the right inmate, I asked if he knew by name the mechanic who worked on my tractor. He answered yes, it was his dad.

I then told him that his dad wanted me to visit and that his dad loved him. At that, the young inmate immediately came to tears. He had been in jail for eleven months and thought his whole family had forgotten him. No one had contacted him at all. He had even considered suicide. Now, at least he knew his dad was thinking about him. He asked if I could tell his dad that he loved him too. I told him I'd do that. Afterward, we had a long and worthwhile conversation.

I later emailed his dad, telling him that his stepson loved him as well. I suggested that the mechanic make some time to go visit his stepson and gave him his stepson's location. He was very grateful and promised he'd find the time.

Now, here's the heart of the matter. Had my tractor not failed, I would never have met this particular mechanic, nor would I have found his stepson. The father-stepson reconnection would never have been made. And maybe because of my broken tractor, just maybe, a suicide was prevented.

You see, the Holy Spirit broke my tractor, and no matter how many visits it took, the tractor would not be repaired until the mechanic had the courage to mention that his stepson was incarcerated.

God indeed is working actively in our lives, and He won't stop until we are safely with Him. All that's required is for us to be aware of His presence and respond with gusto.

Edward Yrisarri Jr, a three-time combat veteran (Korean War), is an electrical engineering graduate (University of New Mexico) and a registered professional engineer. During his working career, he served as an Extra Ordinary Minister of the Holy Eucharist, bringing communion to the terminally ill, hospital ICU, homebound, assisted living, and convalescent homes. After retiring, he worked as a volunteer Catholic chaplain, ministering and teaching certificate religious classes in Texas county jails and state penitentiaries. He has also served as a spiritual advisor. Contact him at **wcbd1@verizon.net.**

Thoughts to Ponder
from The Holy Spirit Broke My Tractor

1. God often uses difficult situations to accomplish His plan.

2. Always be aware of God's presence and divine appointments.

3. God's love penetrates prison bars.

When have you experienced a divine appointment?

Where can I go from your Spirit? Where can I flee from your presence? — Psalm 139:7

Poor Choices

by Donna Banfield

I'm Donna, and I'm an alcoholic.

Ah, wait—wrong meeting.

Seriously, this is how I introduced myself for a period of time, because it was my life. I went to meetings, got a sponsor, did the steps, and even became a sponsor.

It was a struggle every day. When I finally allowed the Lord back into my life, He took the desire away, praise God.

My story began July 30, 1957, when I was born to two alcoholic parents. My mother was just a child, and my dad was twice her age. She was pregnant five times in six years. I was the firstborn, then she had a miscarriage, and later she had a baby girl who only lived a few hours. Following that, she gave birth to my brother and later, my sister.

One day, my parents took us to Mama and Papa's house. They dropped us off—and forgot to come back. They divorced soon after, and I think my mom moved to Florida. I saw my dad a lot, because we were at his mom and dad's. However, my mom's visits were few and far between.

Mama was an invalid. She had a stroke when I was a baby. She could walk if someone helped her up and supported her for balance. So Papa had an invalid wife and three small children to take care of. Mom eventually came back and got my baby sister. It was just too much for Papa.

One of the joys I look forward to in Heaven is thanking Papa for all he did and apologizing for being so bratty at times. I remember him saying, "Little girl, you'll regret that one day." My smart-aleck response was, "No, I won't." He was right.

I also look forward to walking all over Heaven with Mama. I can see her walking purposely, with her arms swinging. It makes me smile to think of it.

Mom and Dad actually did me a favor by leaving me with my grandparents. I was raised in a Christian home, something I wouldn't have had otherwise. There's no telling what kind of life I would have had. I do know I wouldn't have the memories of standing in front of Hamilton Chapel, singing, "Will the Circle Be nbroken?" with Papa, or sitting in the front yard under a big old silver maple with Mama, wondering where all "them cars" were going.

It took many years to forgive my parents, especially my mom. I still don't understand how she could have left us, but I don't have to understand. I just have to understand that the Lord loved me then, and He still loves me, even when I feel unloved or unlovable.

When I was sixteen, I went to live with my mom and sister in Virginia. Less than a year later, my mom was shot and killed by her husband, whose phone number I didn't even know. She had left him, and he wanted her back. He was an alcoholic as well. So alcohol had taken another life. My sister and I then went to live with an aunt and uncle on my mom's side of the family. I'm glad, because I would not have been able to spend time with that side of my family if I'd gone back to Mama and Papa's.

After I received my high school diploma, I moved from Kentucky to Middletown, Ohio, to live with my aunt and uncle, who helped Papa as much as they could. My uncle was the pastor of a decent-sized church, and we lived in the parsonage. I have some wonderful memories from that church. It is where I came to know Jesus.

I met my first husband and was married for about a year. I wasn't ready for marriage. I was very immature for my age and just wanted to play house.

After divorce number one, I met and married the father of my children. We were together over twenty years, and during that time I turned to alcohol.

When my two children were little, I took them to church, but my heart wasn't in it. I wasn't living for the Lord, and the alcohol took over. Eventually, there was a time I only lived for the next drink. I was a functioning alcoholic, and I still wonder what all I missed. My husband and I grew apart and divorced. I was scared to death to be alone with two kids. So my brilliant decision was to marry husband number three, with whom I could party. That was our life.

I put my kids through a lot of distress during that time. My thirteen-year-old daughter sounded the alarm saying, "Mom, you've got to do something." Out of the mouths of babes, huh. That's when I got sober and found my way back to church. However, one

168

drunk and one sober person in recovery does not make a marriage. So on to divorce number three after almost three years.

I met husband number four in rehab, and my relationship with him is a story all its own. Maybe one day, I'll be able to face that ten years of my life so I can write it down. It was such a question mark. I don't know one word that covers it, but a "trying time in my life" is a start. For now, we'll fast-forward through divorce number four.

Meanwhile, my relationship with the Lord was hit or miss. There were spurts of time when things were good. Those were the times I was in church, doing the right things and living right. But I just couldn't seem to stick with it.

I was always letting a man come between me and my walk with God. I never allowed myself time to meet the right kind of man. I felt I must have someone right away, and I never waited for the Lord to put me with His choice. If you don't wait on the Lord, the devil is so quick to send who you think you need.

Today I believe, if the Lord puts someone in my life, it will be a man who not only goes to church but is involved in his church and lives fully for the Lord. If I've used up my allotment of men, I fully understand.

I was raised in church, so I knew and still know that I need Jesus Christ in my life. I chose times in my life to ignore Him and do what Donna wanted. Man, what a mistake. I messed my life up so many times and in so many ways—but most dramatically with alcohol and men.

My life wasn't getting any better my way, and I needed help—a different kind of help than I had tried before. The meetings, talking with friends, seeing psychologists, or just choking it all down wasn't working.

Because none of these things gave me relief, I was empty inside. I kept trying to fill the void with anything I could grab onto—anything except God. I was miserable, and nothing proved satisfying. I now know why. I needed the Lord in my life. Previously, I didn't want to give up other things to serve Him.

As you can see, I made many poor choices. None of them were God-centered. My first thought is to say that I regret those decisions, but would I be where I am today if I could change the past? Would I be the Christian woman that I am now and have peace and contentment in my life? Would I be willing to step out of my comfort zone and allow the Lord to work through me? I don't think so. I believe I had to travel this bumpy road to get where I am today.

I look back and would like to say that I was clueless, but I knew what I was doing. I was stubborn, because I wanted things my way (and that worked out well, didn't it?). Was I blind? Yes and no. I knew I was doing wrong, but I was blind to how good things could be with God. "Just plain stupid" is probably the best description of me. Thankfully, God has forgiven all my sins, and He has marvelous plans for me. And for you!

Isn't that amazing? All we must do is ask.

He paid for our sins, and He's waiting for us to respond. I don't even like to think about how I hurt Him when I was living in sin, knowing I was doing wrong.

I tried to make deals with Him. "Hey God," I said. "I'm not a bad person. I'm not hurting anyone intentionally. I love You, and I go to church sometimes. So surely You'll let me into Heaven. I don't think I'm the first person who has tried to wheel and deal herself into Heaven. And I probably won't be the last."

But none of this brought me peace. I needed to allow the Lord to fill my soul with His Holy Spirit. And praise God, I finally have. By my doing this, He has taken away my desire for alcohol and wrong men. He has given me peace of mind. He has allowed me to be content with myself. He filled my emptiness with His goodness. I am happy. Some groups don't believe or want you to even say that the desire for alcohol can be lifted. But I'm here to tell you that through Christ, anything is possible.

I'm not saying I'm cured. It's an illness in my body that can't be removed. If I choose to pick up another bottle, I'll be right back where I left off. You don't get to start over as if it never happened. I know. I relapsed back in 2004 after two years of sobriety. After one month, I was back in detox in worse shape than when I first became sober. However, the bottle can't seduce me the way it once did. God has taken its power away. I haven't had a drink since 2004, and I don't know if that would be true if I hadn't allowed God back into my life. I don't even know that I would have my children and grandchildren in my life. I believe they would have turned away from me. And justifiably so.

I have stopped trying to guess where I would be today if I had continued the way I was living. I don't know whether I would even be alive. That's not me anymore. Hallelujah!

Since I've moved to Texas and have found the perfect church, I can't believe I wasted so many years on worldly things that meant nothing. Poor choices. And speaking of perfect churches, yes I know nothing on Earth is perfect, but some things are close. My church suits me perfectly. After moving here, I visited a half-dozen churches before I found home. It is so important to be where you're supposed to be.

I'm not trying to kid myself or anyone else. Life isn't perfect, and it never will be here on Earth. But I can accept the imperfections and be grateful for all His goodness and grace He bestows on me. I so look forward to Heaven.

I couldn't have any of this peace in my life if I hadn't asked God to forgive and save me. I think we got the better end of the deal. Jesus had to die on the cross for us. We must only ask for His salvation. Oh, the pain He went through, and it's so simple and painless for us. If you earnestly pray to Him, your life will be new and oh so blessed.

My most frequent prayer is that my family will come to Christ. I want *everyone* to go to Heaven. The alternative is awful. Our time here on Earth is just a flash. This is nothing. Eternity is our reason to live. It is all that matters.

The day my obituary becomes my change-of-address card, I want my family to smile and say, "She's walking all over Heaven with her mama and papa. She and Papa are singing, and Mama's walking everywhere. They're rejoicing.

If you want that peace of mind here on Earth that you'll live eternally in Heaven, just ask. It's this simple: "Lord, I've sinned. Forgive me. Amen."

Donna Banfield *is an aspiring writer, who is currently writing a book of fiction, as well as an autobiography. Her great joy is traveling to see her children and grandchildren. Her son, daughter-in-law, and grandson live in Dayton, Ohio. Her daughter, son-in-law, and three grandchildren live in McKinney, Texas. She is active in her church and desires to be an inspiration to everyone she meets. Donna can be reached at* ***Quilter9Patch@aol.com.***

Thoughts to Ponder
from Poor Choices

1. Temptation enters through a small crack but leaves a wide pit.

2. Submit your choices to the Lord for approval.

3. Nothing fills the void that God created in us for Himself.

What is your process for decision-making?

But when you are tempted, he will also provide a way out so that you can endure it. — 1 Corinthians 10:13

The Battle of My Life
by Itohan Osawe

The battle of my life started before my conception. My dad, a smart industrious businessman, was married and had two beautiful daughters. It was no secret that while he studied overseas, he lived a promiscuous life. As a result, he fathered three children out of wedlock before marrying his mistress in Nigeria. Despite my dad's behavior, things seemed to go well for him and his family. They had mansions, a business, and were well-to-do. There was just one problem—his wife had no male child. That was a big problem in Nigeria. Back then, the male child was the one to inherit the father's title and wealth and take the role as the father figure after the passing of his father. He was supposed to keep the family name going from one generation to the next, because the female child would eventually get married, live with her husband, and take on her husband's name. So a male child was imperative, seen as the pride of the home.

My mom was a young nursing student from a very well-to-do family. She was previously married and had been told she couldn't have children. She was minding her own business when her path crossed with my dad's. After that, everything changed. The acquaintance turned into a relationship that became a full-blown affair. After being told by multiple doctors she was barren and could never have children, she found out she was pregnant with a male child. Despite the way it happened, this pregnancy was a miracle.

The news of the pregnancy spread like wildfire and made my dad's wife very uneasy. The thought of another woman having a boy that she had not been able to bear did not set well, so she took matters into her own hands. She found a witch doctor to help her conceive a male child of her own, and he was given carte blanche to use any means necessary. The witch doctor gave her a substance that would help her in her quest. Twenty-four hours after drinking the concoction, my dad found her dead.

The whole town revolted, and her family accused my mom of killing their sister. Terrified for her unborn son's life, she fled. Nearly a month before my brother was born, she returned and was traditionally married to my dad.

Two years later, I was born, and now my story begins at the age of two. I was with my grandmother, whose house had just been built. The railing on the stairs was not yet installed. I curiously wandered toward the stairs and suddenly found myself falling face-down, hitting the bare concrete. I was rushed to the hospital. It's nothing short of a miracle I survived, especially with a lack of proper medical care. The doctor's son, who was the same age as me, had fallen in the same manner that I had, but he died on impact.

During my childhood, I battled low self-esteem, depression, anger, and unforgiveness. My parents were verbally and physically abusive, both to me and to each other. My dad randomly disappeared for months, sometimes years, and when he returned, all he and my mom did was argue, fight, and transfer their anger and aggression toward us children.

Believing what they said about me, I felt worthless—not smart like my brother and sister. My brother, being the firstborn and only male child, was the pride of my mom's life. My younger sister was my mother's last child—her baby. They always said I was going through the middle-child syndrome.

This was no syndrome. The words were real, the actions were real, and my feelings were real. I truly felt my family did not care about me.

Both my siblings performed great in school, and I was never able to pass a class. To my mother, I was that problem child she wanted to do away with, failing in school, always sick with a cold or flu. I was told I was too sickly, and I just wasn't smart. I was also told I lacked common sense, so the question of what I would be when I grew up became a major topic of discussion. My brother's and sister's paths were clear. My brother wanted to be an electrical engineer, which made my mom proud. My sister decided to be a model and a neurosurgeon. There I was without any plan. They concluded that I was not going to amount to anything. I not only accepted those words, but I acted on them.

When it came to friendship, I was known as the one who could never hold on to friends. I asked God what was wrong with me and why I was even born. Higher education was mandatory in my family, so it was determined I would attend college and get a degree in something—anything. After high school, which I failed woefully, I was pushed to college. I failed at that too, so I dropped out and decided to try cosmetology school. I thought I'd found my passion. It took a year, but I finished.

Shouldn't I be happy and proud for the very first time? I had accomplished something, but a feeling of emptiness was still in my heart. I could not explain it. Not even the accomplishment of finishing cosmetology school and passing my licensing exam could fill the void.

I found myself being accepted by the wrong people. I was soon doing what they did—drinking, smoking, and fornicating. I felt that was the way to a fulfilled life. I knew of God, but I never believed He could be real in my life. Because I grew up in church, I also knew some scriptures. However, I never had a real relationship with God and could never understand the whole concept of God sending His Son to die for sinners like me. Not long after I embarked on my reckless lifestyle, I found out I was seven weeks pregnant. Now, I had really brought shame to my family.

The thought of keeping the pregnancy was not an option, and if my parents ever found out, it would be my death. I knew getting an abortion was killing a life. I knew I was doing wrong in the sight of God, but I thought I had no choice.

After the abortion, I felt God would never give me a future child. I was now damaged goods. No one would want to marry me. I remained celibate for a year, and then I was back to my reckless behavior. During my photo shoot for a hair product line, my friend was smoking a new synthetic marijuana. Foolishly, I decided to try it.

After my first puff, I blacked out and fell hard to the ground. I tried to hold on to something, but there was just darkness. After a seeming eternity of falling, I found myself in a cave, hiding from huge, beastly, baby-like creatures in big diapers, walking around with guard sticks like baseball bats. The cave had prisons with different-sized lakes of fire—a very nasty, greasy, dirty place. Someone was tied up to a campfire roaster, and I was going to be next. Fear overwhelmed me.

My eyes opened. I was surrounded by people. They thought I had fainted from the heat, because it was summer. My friends were too scared to tell anyone about the synthetic marijuana, and I never told my friends what I saw while blacked out. The shock didn't last long. I went back to my old life of drinking, partying, and smoking marijuana—real joints, no synthetics.

The emptiness grew deeper. I concluded that all I needed was love. No man wanted to love me. All they did was drug me, rape me, and use me for sex. I thought, *Why not try to get it from a woman?* That did not last very long. I returned to dating men, which led to one heartbreak after another. It seemed as if everyone around me had life and love. Unlike me, they had figured it out.

Not long after one of my heartbreaks, I lost my job. All I had was my savings, which I wanted to invest in my hair business. The guy I was dating was an old high school friend from Nigeria. He wanted to visit me in the States but didn't have the money for his visa. He said he would pay back my loan when he arrived. Although I had reservations about sending him my savings, he had gone to see my parents in Nigeria, and the prospect of marriage looked promising.

The thought of being married and bringing joy to my parents was much greater than any reservation I had. As soon as I sent the money, he changed his phone number. I was duped.

In an attempt to turn a bad situation around, my mother gave my contact information to an old family acquaintance. I was given a proposal for marriage three months after our long-distance relationship. After one year of long-distance courtship, we were married.

Three months later, we decided it would be better if I moved to Nigeria, because my husband was denied a visa. Our marriage was filled with fights, arguments, and keeping scores. We never seemed to get along, and I quickly grew more depressed from the shame. The man I had married was nothing like the one I had dreamed of. I felt trapped. This could not be my life. I had no income, no higher education, and I was living in a foreign country. There was no need for my existence. The negative thinking went on and on.

Four months pregnant, I decided the pain was just too much to bear. Suicide was my only option. I hated my life. I hated my marriage. I hated everything and everyone, because they were the cause of my problems—not me.

When my husband found me trying to kill myself, he said, "If you kill yourself and die, I will marry someone else. Life will go on for me. I will not cry, and I will not miss you."

Those words cut deep. How could my husband not care about me wanting to kill myself?

After the death of my father, my husband was granted a green card. So after three years of living in Nigeria, my husband and I relocated to the United States. We moved in with my husband's friend. I imagined this was what we needed, a fresh start to help my marriage.

But nothing changed. We went through the same problems, but this time in someone else's house. I tried my best to put on an act, to be that good wife, but my husband complained about everything. When he got home from work, he was angry. When I was cooking and the kids were crying, he was angry and yelled for me to take care of them. I felt disrespected and bitter. How could he treat me like this in his friend's house?

I decided to take the kids to live with my mom, who had moved to the United States after the death of my dad. I contemplated getting a divorce, but it wasn't an option. I had no income, and divorce was expensive. After a few months of separation, my husband moved down to stay with us, and we decided to make it work.

Living with my mom and my husband was my breaking point. My husband soon returned to his past behavior of condemning, criticizing, and complaining about everything I did. My mom was there to support him, so it felt like déjà vu.

I found out that my mom had been unfaithful to my dad six months before he died. She was still having an affair during the time of the funeral preparation. This information changed my whole life.

When I was growing up, my mom always told us that my dad was delusional for accusing her of committing adultery. She made it known that she was the one providing for the family, not my dad. She told us anything to make us think bad about him. We grew up thinking our dad did not love us, that he did not provide for his family. We knew he was womanizer, because after my mom he married another woman in the States and fathered five children with her. One could say to some degree, he didn't provide for us, but he was not delusional when he accused my mom of committing adultery and turning his children against him. I could understand if my mom hadn't been a pastor and humanitarian. She had committed adultery for more than ten years with a married man.

Living together with my mother and husband was one of my biggest challenges. I was either fighting with my husband or my mother. I was tired of fighting. I was in pain, and I needed help. I had failed at life. Depression, anger, and violence was my life. I wanted it all to go away.

On October 7, 2017, I decided to take my life. Nothing was going to stop me. Little did I know that would be the day my whole life would change. After another evening of fighting and arguing, everyone had fallen asleep but me. I was in my closet rolled up in a ball, crying my eyes out. I went to the kitchen and took the sharpest knife. As tears filled my eyes, I asked God, "Why did you create me?" I closed my eyes and thought, *Don't think about it. Just do it.* The plan was to stab myself multiple times really fast. That would surely get the job done.

I raised the knife to finish the job.

"Stop!" the voice said.

Stop? There's no stopping. This is the solution to all my pain. I can't stop.

"Do you want to spend the rest of your life in Hell?"

"No," I said.

"What about the two boys I gave you? Do you really want them to grow up motherless?"

As I thought about my sons and how committing suicide might affect them, I knew my suicide was not what I wanted, for their sake. But how could I go on? I couldn't live another day like this. I was tired.

Then He said, "Come to me, all you who are weary and burdened, and I will give you rest. Take my yoke upon you and learn from me, for I am gentle and humble in heart, and you will find rest for your souls. For my yoke is easy and my burden is light" (Matthew 11:28-30).

Tears rolled down my cheeks as the knife dropped to the floor. I fell to my knees, sobbing, and surrendered my life to Jesus. Immediately, a weight lifted from me. For my whole life, I had tried to live on my own terms, but it led to a place of empty brokenness. Only because of the love and grace of God over my life, I had not been consumed.

As I sobbed, I felt comforted. My emptiness and my

nothingness had led me to a place of total brokenness. In brokenness, I was guided to total surrender to my heavenly Father and Jesus Christ. And now, He could beautifully put me back together and use me as His vessel. I understood, and it was beautiful. I lay in silence for the very first time in my twenty-eight years. I finally understood why He had created me.

After surrendering my life to God, working every day to study His Word and follow His instructions, my whole life transformed. I am no longer depressed, angry, or bitter. My faith in God has quadrupled. I now have a clear picture and direction for what God wants me to do. The joy and peace I have can't be explained, nor can it be shaken. The joy I have for the Lord and my fellow brothers and sisters in Christ is contagious. I no longer blame anyone for the wrong decisions I have made, but I accept them. By the grace of God, I participate in changing what I can change.

My marriage is not perfect, but compared to where it was, it is thriving. I focus on being a submissive and God-fearing wife and mother. I am more open to criticism, and when it hurts too much, I go to my prayer closet and talk to my heavenly Father. Through it all, I have learned more through humility. I have also learned through self-examination. I ask if my conduct and speech is pleasing and in accordance with God's Word. If it is not, I humbly take steps to change, with the help of the Holy Spirit. I was in the battle of my life, but now I know Who to go to—the One who loves to fight our battles, my heavenly Father.

Itohan Osawe is only a vessel instructed to minister healing, hope, deliverance, direction, and love to the world through writing and content creation. When she is not working, she serves her family and the church. She enjoys cooking new scrumptious recipes for her family and reading. You can find her at ScripturesLedLife.com.

Thoughts to Ponder
from The Battle of My Life

1. The power of life and death is in the power of the tongue.

2. When we speak the Word of God into our lives, our situations can be transformed.

3. God has created a special destiny for each of us.

> **How has God used a painful situation in your life to minister to others?**

But rejoice inasmuch as you participate in the sufferings of Christ, so that you may be overjoyed when his glory is revealed. — 1 Peter 4:13

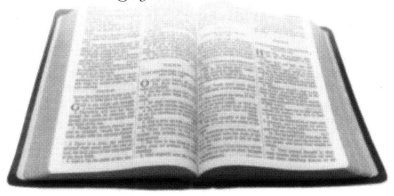

The Gift of Music
by Melinda Propes

I love to sing, and I love being surrounded by others who sing—in a setting where my voice can blend with beautiful melodies offered in worship. There's a debate these days among church-going folk as to what style of music is best in worship, contemporary praise songs or old-fashioned hymns. To me, it doesn't matter much, as I like them both, but if forced to choose, I have to go with hymns. It's hard to beat "Amazing Grace."

One of my early memories is of singing along with Elvis Presley on the radio. Imagine a three-year-old child's version of "Nothing but a Hound Dog." It probably wasn't very good, but apparently I got enough of the words right to make the adults around me laugh.

As an elementary-school-age child, I stood next to my mother in church, listening to her sing hymns like "The Old Rugged Cross" and "This Is My Father's World." I thought she sounded like an angel, which must be where my love affair with music first began in earnest—that and listening to Andy Williams and Johnny Mathis records on our big clunky family stereo where the moon river was wider than a mile. I wanted to play the piano, but we didn't own one or have money for such a purchase. Music education would have to wait.

By the time I started middle school, or junior high as we called it in those days, my parents had formed a good friendship with the neighbors down the street. Both were music majors. One was the band director of the middle school where my siblings and I later attended, and the other was the choir director at a local church.

God's invisible hand was at work, but I didn't know it yet. Because of this musical friendship, my parents were convinced that my brother, sister, and I should join the middle-school band. My brother went first, choosing the clarinet. My sister followed with the flute. I wanted to play flute too, but my sister had already claimed that territory, making it off-limits. Since my family seemed to be stuck on woodwinds, I chose the oboe, a sad, sometimes forlorn-sounding instrument. It suited me though, and I learned to love it despite its melancholy sound.

Participation in band taught me valuable music skills, like how to read notes, keep time, and sight-read music. Typically, only one or two oboe players are in a band, but my band had three to four. I was almost always last chair in my section, mainly because I had no confidence when called to play individually. I was shy in those days, so I didn't mind being last. It was a "safe" place to be. Though I might be able to play well on my own during practice, a bad case of nerves always took over during chair tests, causing my playing to stumble. I also developed a terrible and lasting case of performance anxiety after one failed attempt at an oboe solo during a concert. My big chance and I flubbed it. Better leave the solo performing up to other people and just keep hiding comfortably in the background.

I continued playing the oboe through high school, then switched to the alto saxophone in the junior college band. The alto saxophone and I never really clicked, so I was glad to give it up after a year and a half, when I transferred to a four-year college. There, my formal music education faded. My oboe was relegated to the top shelf of my closet, where it still sits, a treasured but unused relic.

During my college years, I had a short stint of teaching myself to play guitar on an old, not very good instrument I found in the back of my brother's closet. With little confidence in my singing ability, I practiced only while alone in the house. I didn't get very far in that venture. But never fear, God is in the business of second chances.

My next music venture came when I was a young married woman. My husband and I joined a church shortly after we married, and before long we found ourselves looking for ways to fit in and serve. The logical place for me to start was the choir. I remembered how much I loved listening to my mother sing those hymns in church. My band background helped a bit, but I had very little choral experience to fall back on.

My first year truly was a "learn as you go" kind of thing, but before long I fell head over heels in love with choral music. Wednesday night choir practice became a highlight of my week. Singing in the church choir lasted several years, until the busyness of parenting two kids caused me to drop out. Now it was my turn to pass my love of music to my kids. I raised them on Disney songs and musicals like "Phantom of the Opera" and "Les Misérables." Different music from my mother's, but the same effect.

When you get out of the habit of something, it can be a challenge to pick it back up. Just ask my oboe, sitting on the closet shelf, gathering dust. Such was the case for me after dropping out of choir for fifteen years. If not for the encouragement of a faithful friend, I might never have found the courage to sing in a choir again. My friend was tired of hearing me say I was thinking about it. "We're going," she said. Yes, she joined the choir so I would. What a friend!

Singing in choir was like coming home after being away a long time. The familiar faces from the old choir weren't there, but the music welcomed me back like a long-lost friend. It was like rediscovering how much you love chocolate or finding your lost pair of comfortable old house shoes. However, this choir was different from the one before. The director was more high-energy than I was used to, and the group was two to three times larger. Rehearsals moved along quickly despite the difficulty of the music. At first, all my insecurities came roaring back. Those high notes seemed a lot higher, and my tones seemed flatter. I gave myself a weekly lecture just to keep from giving up. My singing finally improved, and my confidence increased—just a little bit. I had found a spot in my new church choir.

Several years later, my now adult, newly married daughter decided to join the choir herself, following in my footsteps. Emily had participated in school choirs throughout her growing-up years, and I knew what a talented singer she was—like my mother. Having my daughter join me was a dream come true. Near me each week, I enjoyed her company and listened to her lovely voice. My daughter was a better singer, with more training and more natural talent. However, what she had in talent, she lacked in confidence. Sounds rather familiar, doesn't it? Sadly, I admit to having passed along that unfortunate trait to her.

At Wednesday night choir practice, the director of small ensembles often passed around a sign-up sheet for volunteers, which I always passed along without hesitation. That was for more-talented people like my daughter, Emily, not me. I noticed her passing that sign-up clipboard with barely a glance. So it was my job to help her see that she should be volunteering. That's what mothers are for, right?

One night as the clipboard was passing by, I said to her, "You really ought to put your name on that list. You're good enough to sing in an ensemble. Why don't you go ahead and sign it?" What a good, smug feeling I had at that piece of motherly advice. The response I got was wholly unexpected, however.

My grownup daughter calmly and confidently looked me in the eye and said, "I will if you will."

That was not what I had bargained for. Over the years, I overcame my fear of public speaking and praying out loud before a group. I no longer had a morbid fear of speaking into a microphone, and had gained confidence in teaching my Sunday school class. Singing in a small ensemble, however, was definitely not on my list of conquered fears. It was something I never intended to do, being quite sure I did not have the ability. Every choir needs background singers, and I was happy being one of those. You know, filler for the other, better voices.

Emily remained firm, saying, "I'm not going to sign up if you're not."

I was trapped. I really wanted her to do it, but apparently I had to join her to make it happen.

"Okay, just this once."

We put our names on the list. I don't know how she felt, but I did so with fear and trembling. After a few rehearsals, the day came when we were to sing. With trembling knees and butterflies in my stomach, I stood with Emily and the others in our small group to sing before the church in worship. I didn't die of fright.

I breathed a sigh of relief.

Oh good, that's done, and now I can move on. Emily should feel more confident next time, and I won't have to do it again.

Actually, things didn't quite turn out that way. Yes, Emily did share her talent by singing in a number of other ensembles before she eventually dropped out of choir to become mother to her small children. I have continued to sing in my church choir, in both the larger group and in smaller ensembles. Over time, I have grown to know that I do have the ability to contribute in small ensembles. I actually enjoy it quite a lot. It's a little ironic, isn't it? When I thought I was being so smart to encourage my daughter, she was the one who encouraged me. Taking it further, God was the One who encouraged us both.

The Bible says in 1 Thessalonians 5:11, "Therefore encourage

184

one another and build each other up, just as in fact you are doing." That's what my daughter did for me.

God is relentless in leading His children down the path He wants them to go. It seems that whenever the Holy Spirit and I conquer one thing, He moves me on to tackle the next challenge. For whatever reason, music seems to frequently be part of my life's experience.

A few years ago, my musical journey took a new turn when my husband and I took up playing the ukulele. We joined a ukulele "choir" at a church not our own and made a whole new group of music friends. Recently, I helped start a ukulele choir at my own church and can only chalk that up to being a sign of God's amazing sense of humor.

Lastly, several years ago, I found myself confronting another long-held fear of individually singing into a microphone. I had avoided any chance of that happening until I found myself on stage next to my adult son, singing praise songs with his band and leading worship at a pilgrimage retreat.

Now, I have learned to never say "never," because as soon as I do, it seems that's the direction I am led to go. The adventure continues, and only God knows what will happen next.

The gift of music keeps on giving.

Melinda Propes is a new author of inspirational faith stories. Previous careers include working as a draftsman/technical illustrator, a psychologist's assistant, as well as owning and operating a longarm quilting business. Melinda loves to travel with her husband of forty-two years and enjoys spending time with her two children and their families. She believes in giving back to her community and regularly volunteers at a local food pantry.

For more information, please contact Melinda at MPropez@tx.rr.com.

Thoughts to Ponder
from The Gift of Music

1. If it would please God, do what you fear.

2. God is in the business of second chances.

3. We have the power to influence other people, so use this God-given power to further His Kingdom.

> ***In what area might God be calling you to trust Him more and to follow where He leads?***

He put a new song in my mouth,
a hymn of praise to our God. — Psalm 40:3

Thunders of Pain
by Irene Cayong Robertson

It was a routine doctor's office visit. The internist would simply give me a reminder and a few medical instructions on diet, exercise, and the continued intake of my prescribed hypertension medicines. I thought this would be like all my previous checkups. Instead, my world was shattered on that cool morning in October.

As I sat on the examination table, the doctor gave me a physical exam. I chatted away about the good things that I did health-wise, that I exercised sometimes and tried to stay away from sweets. She nodded and muttered, "Hmmm," a few times as she continued her examination.

She looked over my eyes and up my nose. She poked a cone-shaped instrument into both my ears, then pressed a beige slab of thin wood onto my tongue to check my throat and tonsils. Apparently, nothing there was significantly wrong, because the doctor didn't say a word. As if she was bringing the stethoscope to life, she thumped it in one of her palms, then placed the cold instrument on my neck. It seemed like an eternity as she went up and down my neck like a concert pianist on the keys of a delicately tuned and aged grand Steinway. Finally, she removed the "stet" (a term medical people use), and let it hang on her shoulders. She looked at me square in the eyes and calmly said, "I need to run a sonogram on your carotids. It's just a simple test to make sure everything is okay." Unwillingly, I walked over to the sonogram room, where a far-eastern-looking man, speaking broken but understandable English, kindly and professionally gave me instructions to lie still.

After the test was completed, I overheard bits and pieces of his consult with my internist. Because he used grave tones, I sensed something unpleasant was coming. Then the internist read the report. "I'm referring you to a vascular surgeon."

What? I felt myself shouting inside my mind, but no words came out. *No! No! No! I don't want to see one.* After I finally found my voice, I exclaimed, "A vascular surgeon. You know surgeons always operate."

Being an operating room nurse, I knew its implications. I was familiar with carotid surgeries. I assisted in them and had been the advocate for patients undergoing that procedure. Patients who have this type of surgery are in danger of experiencing a stroke while on the operating table, and there is also the chance that the clamps the surgeons use will malfunction. Patients can lose their voices or bleed to death. I knew enough about the aspects of that surgery, "pre," "during," "post," and all the potential complications. The data was so traumatizing, like sharp, pointed steel tongs piercing my brain.

I called my husband as soon as I closed the door of the doctor's reception area. I was suppressing any sign of emotional collapse. I felt his support and understanding, and he reassured me that he would take care of me. Of course, God would too.

I procrastinated setting up an appointment with the vascular surgeon, even though I knew full well, because of my carotid issue, I could have a TIA (transient ischemic attack) or a full-blown debilitating cerebral stroke. I inched up to 90 percent blockage in my carotid arteries. Finally, the day came.

This desperate emergency brought me to Heaven's door. Yes, I had to undergo a Bilateral Carotid Endarterectomy. Yes, I will do it after the Christmas holidays. Yes, there are no other alternatives. Yes, I will have tightening and two scars in my neck. Yes, I'll feel better with the blood flow going into my brain, rather than hearing the whooshing sound of palpitations, like the ocean's waves undulating on the seashore. Yes, there will be truckloads of pain. However, by doing the surgery, the chance of a stroke occurring diminishes, and I'll get fifteen to twenty more years of living.

Being a Christian, I knew within my spirit that God wanted something. Yet I rebelled like a two-year-old with relentless tantrums. I kicked and shrieked inside my mind during the day, but my eyes turned upward to the sky whenever the dusk of the evening approached. Since I have a privileged relationship with God the Father, Jesus the Son, and the Holy Spirit, I know I can tell Them anything that goes on in my life. I questioned Him without reservation.

Why? Why me, Lord? Such an inconvenience, Lord.

I had things to do. I had to work. I needed to pay the bills. Confusion pressed in. Fear touched the hemlines of my mind. No verses seeped into my senses, no signs, no answers, no explanations to be found.

I felt Jesus was standing by, waiting for me to have an in-depth talk with Him.

One day while preparing for work, I looked at the mirror. I felt the day was different. A song took form on the blank music sheet of my reasoning. It was an old familiar tune, a hymn from yesteryear that I enjoyed listening to: "I Surrender All." I finally said, "Lord, may Your will be done in my life."

I'll endure the surgeon's blade as he removes the offending plaque to better my health. I will glorify God in this manner and honor the doctor's wish. I will trust my surgeon and be convinced that he knows what he is doing, that God can get me through this. Yes, I surrender all. Right at that moment, I felt at peace. My life verse, which has been my mainstay, overrode any qualms or anxiety. In John 14:27, Jesus says, "Peace I leave with you; my peace I give you. I do not give to you as the world gives. Do not let your hearts be troubled and do not be afraid."

I wasn't afraid anymore.

The peace I felt defied any explanation. It was not a superficial or fleeting feeling. I considered it a God-given grace.

The surgery was safe and successful. The doctors, nurses, and all medical personnel treated me well, far better than expected. My husband was at my side. Friends, co-workers, Bible study groups, and family members prayed and visited. It was all because of God's loving mercy and grace.

When strangers ask about my neck, I tell them I had surgery, and thanks to God and Jesus (pointing my forefinger upward), I'm alive. Most people nod and acknowledge that yes, there is a God. *Dios es Bueno! Sí, Sí.* Then, if they feel chatty, I tell them more about God's love.

Even as a Christian, I am not immune to fear or anxious thoughts. Those emotions can overwhelm. But when in total abandonment and surrender, I simply lay all the disquiet of my life, health, and future into the encircling arms of Jesus where healing, mercy, love, and peace abound. No price can match the certain peace that comes with surrender.

Irene Cayong Robertson was born in Banaue Ifugao Province,

Philippines. She is a Registered Nurse by profession, choir member, and poet. Her poem, The Anatomy of an Aging Woman, *placed second in A Galaxy of Verse 2017. One of her poems,* How, *was published in the PST Summer Conference Anthology 2018. Irene maintains membership with Mockingbird Poetry Society, was elected Vice President of the Poetry Society of Texas, and is a member of the National Federation of State Poetry Societies, Inc. She resides in Little Elm, Texas, with her husband, John. Contact her at* **YRanie@att.net.**

Thoughts to Ponder
from Thunders of Pain

1. Don't ask why. Ask how you can use this for God's glory.

2. As a Christian, we are not immune to fear or anxious thought.

3. Surrendering all to Jesus is the best way to live.

What worries do you need to give to Jesus?

When you pass through the waters, I will be with you;
and when you pass through the rivers, they will not sweep over you.
When you walk through the fire, you will not be burned;
the flames will not set you ablaze. — Isaiah 43:2

God's Hand
by Judy Litalien

If it weren't for the hand of God, I would have been dead at age seventeen. If you have ever wondered if God is real, keep reading, because this story is for you.

I grew up in the Rio Grande Valley in the city of McAllen. My family went to church every time the doors were opened, Sunday morning, Sunday night, and Wednesday night—with a few other times thrown in for good measure. My mother came from a long line of believers, but my dad did not grow up in the church. He always went with us, but he was not the spiritual leader of the family. He was baptized when I was about seven years old.

My brother is a year older than me. My sister was born when I was eleven. My parents called me the "built-in babysitter." I probably changed more diapers than both my parents combined. They were so busy, I took care of my sister from the time she was born.

Until I was a little older, I thought most families were like mine. The hypocrisy was most evident to me at church. You see, on the way to church every Sunday, I heard all the church gossip and the suppositions of what might happen that day. Sometimes my parents were in a heated argument, but the minute the car doors opened, we put on our happy faces and pretended to be the Cleavers from *Leave It to Beaver*. All the way home after church, we were back with the same bantering, with complaints about the preaching or the dress somebody wore.

Participating in church was still a happy time, because I had the best Bible teachers. They took an interest in me and not only taught me about Jesus but also were the hands and feet of Jesus to me. Something told me that the faces they put on at church were the same they wore all week. I wanted to belong to *that* family. If you are a teacher, you may not realize the difference you make in the lives of children. You never know when you might have a child in your class, like I was, who is watching and learning by your example, because they don't have a good example at home.

You see, my mom was very abusive, mostly verbally, but for the smallest thing she was known to pull a switch off the tree at a moment's notice. She told me I was too fat, that no one would want to be my friend, and I would never amount to anything. Dad just didn't want to be bothered. He wanted to come home from work, read the newspaper, watch TV, and not have to do anything else. Mom ran the house, and we were to follow her orders.

When I was ten, I was baptized. Like the day was yesterday, I remember the sound of my sandals slapping against the floor as I walked the long aisle to the front. Everyone was singing "Just as I Am," and I can still picture the floral dress I was wearing. I wanted to belong to Jesus. Some people baptized at a young age may not have known what they were doing, but I knew. I knew I was His.

When I look back, I realize that God had His hand on me and was preparing me. He developed a relationship with me early on so when the storms of life hit hard, I had a lifeline. I read my Bible, I prayed, and I tried to be the very best girl I could be. I hadn't heard about grace, so I was trying to work my way to Heaven. I was the good daughter who obeyed her parents. I made straight A's in school and never caused trouble. My bedroom was the cleanest room in the house. I wanted to please everyone—my parents, my teachers, my friends, and God. But no matter how many A's I came home with, my parents were never pleased. However, as the years passed, my relationship with God continued to grow stronger.

On December 10, when I was seventeen, my world turned upside down. My school-teacher mother was driving four of her students to a nearby town to deliver gifts to a four-year-old girl with cancer, who was not expected to live until Christmas. Her family was poor, so the school had collected food for them. On the little two-lane road, a man lost control of his car and plowed head-on into my mom's car. After an hour, they finally got my mom out of the car. She had a head injury, collapsed lungs, and multiple broken bones. A couple days later, she slipped into a coma. I asked, *Why would God let this happen when she was doing something good?*

When my mother came out of the coma, she was partially paralyzed on her left side. She eventually came home and was immobile for several months until the casts were taken off her legs. After school and weekends, I took care of her, as well as my six-year-old sister. My mom could remember things from twenty years ago, but she couldn't remember what our house looked like or where things were. She didn't even recognize her own clothes. I kept busy doing the cooking, cleaning, and grocery shopping—and I also had to keep up with my homework.

My mom started going into rages, accusing anyone nearby of doing things or moving things around just to confuse her. I was usually the one nearby. My brother had his own vehicle, so he stayed gone most of the time. My dad came home later and later at night, but he expected a hot meal on the table whenever he got home. He didn't want to hear what had been going on, and he refused to defend me during my mother's attacks.

One night our minister, Randy Daw, came to encourage us. He told us to "look for the light at the end of the tunnel." I didn't see any light. Doctors kept telling us it was just the head injury. Once the swelling went down, she would be back to her normal self. They didn't know the horrors we were living with at home. They saw my mother as a poor victim of a tragedy, and her family was not being supportive enough of her fragile condition.

In one of her rages, my mother was determined to get out of bed and walk to the bathroom with casts on both legs. She was super strong when she went into a rage, and I was afraid she would injure herself further if she fell. And I wouldn't be able to get her up off the floor. So I held her in bed while my little sister called one of the church elders, who lived the next road over.

Mr. and Mrs. Taylor came over, and they saw what was happening. In that "don't ask, don't tell" era, people didn't share their personal business. After putting on our church faces for our whole lives, we knew the routine well and did not tell anyone. But without having to explain, the Taylors had seen enough. Before they left, Mrs. Taylor took the house key off her key ring, pressed it into my hand, and told me I could make myself at home at their house anytime, no questions asked. They were Jesus to me that day, and on the difficult days that followed, I took them up on their generous offer.

My mother's rages became worse, especially after she became mobile again. Due to her head injury, we didn't know if she knew what she was doing and could be held responsible for her actions. When something set her off, we were never prepared. She would suddenly come after my sister and me with a butcher knife, a meat tenderizer, a hammer, or whatever she could get her hands on. We ran to get away from her. I took the screen off my bedroom

194

window so we could lock the door and quickly climb out the window. She was always right on our heels. We hid in the orchard behind our house until my dad got home. These events replayed in my nightmares for years.

At night, I sat in the rocking chair in my room and cried, but God was there. I felt like He had his arms wrapped around me, holding me. He probably cried with me. I felt His comfort. No promises for something better. Just comfort. I couldn't tell our family secrets to anyone, so I told God all about it all, even though He already knew.

We lived on a paved road, unlike others in the area, so our road was usually very busy with traffic. As I was driving my mother to her physical therapy appointment, I had just pulled onto the road and was headed toward town when she went into one of her rages. She frantically searched the glove compartment for some kind of weapon and found a ball point pen. With her raging strength, she punctured my leg with the pointed end and lodged it there. She clawed at me, pulled my hair, and grabbed the steering wheel, fighting for control. From the back seat, my sister tried to fight her off me. With God's help, I turned the car around and went back home. If there had been traffic on the road, if it hadn't been for God watching over me, I would have been dead.

Miraculously, I graduated from high school and went to a local university for my freshman year of college. I was going to school, working, and returning home to take care of my family. I was able to postpone my Abilene Christian University (ACU) scholarship for one year. When my sophomore year rolled around, I left for ACU. I was a fish out of water there. I was used to taking care of a family of five, and suddenly I didn't know what to do with myself. I missed my little sister like crazy and worried about her.

This was when I met Jim. He brought me out of my shell and taught me how to laugh. He appreciated me and treated me like someone special. He helped me make the transition from caretaker to teenager. I needed him in my life to complete me, a true gift from Heaven. I felt safe telling him things I had never told anyone.

When I took him home with me that summer to meet my family, I realized how much God had protected me. After being away for a while and living a normal life, I had almost convinced myself that things had not been so bad. Then I saw my bedroom door, the beat-up chopped-up door full of knife holes, where slivers of light from the window shone through. The broken lock had held the door just long enough—every time—for us to escape out the window. I knew, if God hadn't protected me, I would have been dead.

Jim and I married in 1986, and it wasn't long before God blessed us with two precious children, Christopher and Jessica. When I first got pregnant, I was afraid I wouldn't be a good mother. I decided all I could do was love them with all my heart, teach them about God, and the rest would work itself out.

When the kids were five and four, we moved from Washington State to the Rio Grande Valley, not far from my mom and dad. A few years earlier, Jim had set my dad up in a business, and now my dad was having health issues. He needed someone to run the business. So Jim went to work for my dad. Things had not really changed with my mother, but time and distance had allowed me to forget how bad it had been. This time we had our own home, and we thought we could insulate ourselves from their problems. A few years passed, and Jim and I realized that we needed to move away. We took a vacation to Dallas to see Jim's mom, and while we were there, Jim went on several job interviews. When we returned home, we had not yet heard back from any of the jobs, so we decided to have a family meeting. We sat with our children and prayed that God would open the right doors. As soon as we finished praying, the phone rang. It was a job offer for a manager position at Braum's. We took it as a sign from God and accepted.

We didn't know how we were going to afford to move to Richardson, but we knew God had a plan. So we started packing. Jim went to work right away, and the kids and I waited for him to find a place for us to live. The church gave us a going-away party and presented us with a money tree. And wouldn't you know, the amount was exactly what we needed to pay for the moving truck. We knew this was a blessing from God.

Shortly after Jim started work, a group of teens came into the restaurant and Jim asked where they were from—part of a youth group from Richardson East Church of Christ led by Dan Stevens. Jim told them we would be moving the next weekend, and that we were looking for a church home. Dan told him about the upcoming Vacation Bible School, took down our address, and invited us to come. Jim was excited to tell us about God's direction once again. Moving day arrived, and Jim and I were tired after the long journey to Dallas. It was going to be another long day unloading the truck. We pulled up and started to unload. Then we heard the doorbell. Four strong teenage boys had come from the youth group to help us unload. God blessed us once again.

A few years passed, and my parents decided to divorce. My brother and I and our families went home one weekend to help my mother pack. The plan was for her to stay with my brother for a month or so, stay with us for a while, and go back and forth so she wouldn't be a burden to anyone. We got her packed up and headed home. Only a couple days later, my sister-in-law called. She didn't know if she could handle my mother. I told her I would come the next weekend to help out. But by Wednesday, things had gotten much worse, and I was asked to come right then. So I headed to Houston. Jim stayed behind with the kids, who were in school. He and the kids would come Friday night.

It was just the way it had been when I was seventeen, living at home. The name calling, hurtful words, and violence. We tried to keep my mother as calm as possible, but it was a losing battle. By the time Jim and the kids arrived, we had a full-blown calamity. We did not want our kids exposed to this. We had to do something. We ended up calling an ambulance to take her to the hospital. She attacked the ambulance drivers. The hospital decided she needed a psychiatric evaluation and made arrangements to transport her to a facility in Palestine.

In the meantime, my brother and I took turns sitting with her in the emergency room. After lunch, I took my turn. As soon as I entered the room, vile, hateful words flowed from my mother's mouth. Restrained, she could not hurt me physically, but she more than made up for it with her words. I sat in the chair with my back to the wall, just praying to God, unwilling to endure this again. And most importantly, I did not want my children to see what I had lived through. Then it felt like God was speaking to me, telling me to open the door. I got up and walked across the room to the door. My mother was triumphant, thinking she had run me off, banished by her insults. But after opening the door, I went back and sat down. The insults stopped. She quietly said, "You think you're so smart, don't you?"

It was then that I knew. All those years we had taken her abuse, because we didn't know she could be held responsible. In that moment, I knew it was all intentional. My eyes were opened to the true evil that resided in her. I knew the words in my head were from God, because I had no idea that opening the door would cause her to stop. My mother had played the victim to outsiders for many years, and she was quite good at it. But to us, she showed her evil side. When I opened the door, she couldn't let the nurses outside the door hear the things she was saying to me—or they would know she was not the victim she was portraying. The realization of what was really going on suddenly became clear. My brother also had a moment when he saw her change right in front of him, just like I had. I believe God revealed that to us. Why then, and not years before, I don't know. Maybe we weren't ready. Maybe we had something we needed to learn first. I don't know, but I do know that God revealed the truth to us that day.

A few days later, doctors told us that my mother had borderline personality disorder, a serious mental illness. She most likely had it from a very young age, but she was able to mask it well. After the head injury, she was no longer able to control it, which was why her rages were so fierce.

My family was never the same. My brother has not fully dealt with it all, going through three marriages in the process. My sister turned to drugs and has been in and out of jail over the years. We have taken her and her children time and time again. My dad remarried and lives in Mexico.

I went through a three-year period when talk with my mother was too painful. But God did not leave me there. He used that time to heal me. Tim Spivey's series on forgiveness made me think about my mother again, and I realized it was time. When I was ready and had finally forgiven her for all that she had done to me, I contacted her. Within six months of that initial contact, I decided I would move my mother up to North Texas near my sister and me. Knowing what she had cost me, Jim questioned whether I wanted to let her back into my life. But I knew it was time. She now lives at Christian Care near our home. I visit her every week. She takes medication that keeps her rages under control, and I have the option of leaving at any time.

My favorite passage is found in Isaiah 43:1–3. "Do not fear, for

I have redeemed you; I have summoned you by name, you are mine. When you pass through the waters, I will be with you; and when you pass through the rivers, they shall not sweep over you. When you walk through fire, you will not be burned; the flames will not set you ablaze. For I am the Lord your God, the Holy One of Israel, your Savior."

God is real. He has never left me. He has been my Protector, my Healer, my Savior, my Encourager, my Friend, my Shelter, and my Lifeline. If it weren't for God, I would have been dead at age seventeen, but instead I share this testimony as a witness to God's hand in my life. I no longer carry the burden of family secrets or lies that were told. I am a child of the King.

Judy Litalien is a statistical analyst. She is married with two grown children and three grandchildren. Judy serves in the technology booth at her church and sings on the praise team. She serves on the committee for Heartfelt Friends and wrote the curriculum for last year's Bible study. She is currently working on next year's study. Judy enjoys reading, crafts, and spending time with her family. She and her husband reside in Garland, Texas. You can reach her at JLitalien86@att.net.

Thoughts to Ponder
from God's Hand

1. You can be the hands and feet of Jesus to someone else.

2. God reveals His truth to us in His perfect timing.

3. There is no need to carry the burden of family secrets and lies.

> ### *What old wound in your life has time healed?*

The righteous person may have many troubles, but the Lord delivers him from them all. — Psalm 34:19

Fearless

by Warren Walters

Occasionally, someone will ask me, "What do you miss the most about being young?" or "What is the one thing you miss from your youth?" Have you ever had that line of inquiry directed at you?

It depends how old you are, I guess—and how old the folks are in whose company you are. It's not a question that the very young even think of. Years ago, as a teen, it never crossed my mind to ask some old guy what he missed the most about being young.

But all of a sudden, it seems you find yourself in that realm. People now find it perfectly acceptable to ask you the question. It's almost like someone hung a sign around your suddenly scrawny neck, saying, "Okay, I'm fair game now. Ask away."

I'm not quite sure how it happened, but here I am, about to enter the back half of my eighty-fourth year. Some people feel at ease to ask, "Warren, what do you miss the most from your youth?"

Depending on where I am at the time and with whom, there can be many kinds of responses—a ready quip to get the company laughing, a short story to stir the memory, a warning, perhaps, that their turn for that question is nigh. Something designed to deflect the conversation from what could possibly be a painful reminder of better times, all dictated by the circumstances at the time.

Or perhaps, one may come up with a list of any number of things that could be missed from those younger days. It could include, for example, some of the sporting accomplishments—perhaps in a variety of sports—that were a highlight of one's younger, stronger days.

Similarly, achieving difficult goals set by "impossible" bosses during the various jobs as one grew in maturity and moved from one position to another. The difficulties associated with successfully combining all those challenges simultaneously with marriage and raising a family. All are legitimate items for such a list, and there would be many more, I'm sure.

Looking back, one wonders how the fuel of youth always seemed to be in an inexhaustible supply. We never questioned it. We just consumed it like it was our God-given right to do so.

However, right now in the cold light of day, when I ask myself that very same question, "What do I miss the most from the days of my youth?" I go through the list of fearless acts with some ruthlessness.

I'm not talking about bravery, you understand. That's different. Being brave isn't a matter of being fearless. Not at all. Bravery is, in fact, doing something "above and beyond the call of duty," despite your fears. Most combat vets will tell you the same thing. Anyone not scared of bullets buzzing by in a battle is bonkers.

The fearlessness I am talking about is different. It is the feeling that wells up inside a youngster's chest when a challenge is issued. Remember?

"Go on, smarty, let's see you make that jump."

"Come on, is that as fast as you can go on that thing?"

"Hey, I thought you could climb. You'll never make it to the top."

"You can't balance on one foot on that thin wire going across that drop, not in those shoes."

How well I recall those times when the adrenaline rushed to my feeble but ever-responsive brain. Always up to the challenge, I never let fear be a factor. Calculate risks? Not me. I had skill. I was daring, had good judgment, and maintained total belief in my own ability. What a putz. Looking back on those days now, considering some of the risks I took, I wonder how I managed to live so long.

And for what reason? Someone dared me to. They challenged me. I believed I was ten feet tall and was totally bullet proof. Even the occasional broken bone didn't cure any of that—it was usually somebody else's fault anyway, right? It could hardly be a miscalculation on my part. "What chu talkin' bout Willis?"

Then, as the bloom of youth faded and I donned the mantle of early manhood, the challenges that came along to test my mettle were no longer a game, no longer a matter of me just trying to go one better than my friends. These challenges, I was finding, were part of life and failure, and they had consequences. So then, risks were indeed calculated and assessed, and wherever possible, circumvented so the job could be done safely. But on occasion, risks had to be accepted in the job, and the job still had to be done. Safely. Because lives were on the line.

I suppose that in almost every line of work there would be some kind of risk involved, should something go wrong during the process. In the financial world, a decimal point in the wrong spot could cost a lot of money. In the construction industry, a miscalculation could see a load-bearing wall collapse when someone tried to hang a window in it. There are potentially many more examples.

In my two areas, the Navy and the steel industry, risks were inevitable to get certain jobs done, but the risks involved were always calculated. Hazards were eliminated, or at least circumvented where possible, and those who were to do the jobs were made aware of the known dangers. Those challenges were absorbed willingly, completely, and yes, fearlessly.

Not now though. Nowadays, I don't even do ladders. But back then, I hung by one hand from the skid of a helicopter while trying to pull a guy out of a drifting boat with the other hand.

Ha! Adrenaline rush? It's overrated.

Now that I have far more yesterdays behind me than tomorrows in front of me, I can afford to "take it easy" and get some young bloke to do the "heavy lifting."

But it's not a nice feeling to no longer be fearless, physically. These days, I only have to stand on the edge of something a bit higher than I am, and the pucker factor is very real. Never used to be. It is unsettling. Balance can be an issue with us "oldies," as some would know. The downer induced by the prospect of a broken hip is always exercising the frontal lobes when we seniors are engaged in any activity more adventurous than getting in and out of a golf cart.

Once upon a time, I used to leap about with the best of 'em, but now, I may leap to a conclusion occasionally, but that's about it. Mind you, I did make a giant leap fairly recently. It was my leap of faith. I went into that one totally blind, but with complete trust that I would not be falling flat on my face. And what a leap it was. All it took was for someone to line me up on the entry way to that narrow path I had heard about, and whammo! There I was, sailing through—what? I was going to say, the air, but that's ridiculous. More like, I was sailing through—and beyond—all the sham, the half-truths, the denials, the mockery, the negativity, the animosity, the anger, the "dim wittedness" of those who just don't get it, to find sure footing on that narrow path that leads to eternal life.

I also found something I thought was irretrievably lost. I found my fearlessness again. Not physically, but spiritually.

At the ripe old age of 78, I was introduced to God's Son. I didn't know Him. I had heard of Him, for sure, and I knew His Dad. In fact, His Dad had kept an eye on me all these years, keeping me out of major trouble. But Jesus? Nah! I had never met Him. That is, until I was led to a Bible-believing church in Hot Springs Village, where I live. Then came that "Whammo!" I mentioned. "Forget the physical fearlessness." I don't need it. Now I have the spiritual fearlessness that allowed me to make that "leap of faith" to become a disciple of the Lord Jesus Christ. My life has just never been so good.

When people greet me asking how I am, my stock answer is always, "Never better." And it's true. They may look at me funny, as if to question that statement coming from an old man, but I qualify it by saying, "No, not on the outside. On the inside." Believers readily understand, 'cause they get it.

I may be old, but I am a kid in Christ, and because of that, I have no fear of the days to come.

Warren Walters was born in New South Wales, Australia, August 1934, served in the Royal Australian Navy for fifteen years, married Margaret, December 1960, and had two children, Grant and Tracie. Margaret died in May of 1997. Warren became a dance host on a cruise ship in December 1998 and met Maria. He relocated to the United States in August 2000 to marry Maria. He moved to Hot Springs Village in May 2005. where Maria died in February 2010. Then Warren met Gail in August of 2011, and she led Warren to the Lord. God's long-term plan was realized.
W3onSeven2012@gmail.com

Thoughts to Ponder
from Fearless

1. No matter what age, you can be a child of God.

2. When we are afraid, remember that God did not give us a spirit of fear.

3. It's not the number of your years but the depth of your love.

> **When was the last time you climbed onto your heavenly Father's lap?**

Gray hair is a crown of splendor; it is attained in the way of righteousness. — Proverbs 16:31

Should I Go or Should I Stay?
by Gwen Burno

Should I go or should I stay? These questions haunted me as I made plans to attend my thirty-fifth high school class reunion on a cruise in the summer of 2017. My emotions were engaged in a tug-of-war as I belabored this decision. My usual razor-sharp decision-making skills abandoned me at a time when I needed them most. My gut leaped in all directions as guilt, pleasure, and devotion took turns vying for my attention.

This gut-wrenching choice involved my oldest brother, Anthony, who was living with lung cancer—or more accurately stated—dying slowly. He had fought a long, hard battle with a disease that our family rightfully declared an enemy. In 2003, this enemy first introduced itself to our family through our father, who was unable to claim an earthly victory. George, my Pops, passed away leaving an indescribable void, like a sinkhole. We hoped never to find ourselves near this abyss again, but there we were, positioned at command attention with the same enemy.

I will never forget receiving the initial news regarding my brother. The flood of emotions poured out and reopened the wounds that had refused to heal with time. Confronted with two choices—either resist the inevitable current or raise the white flag and succumb to the flow—I chose the latter and prayed for a gentle landing. Just in case you don't get the allegory, I am referring to grieving. Those who have experienced the effects of grieving understand that the process operates on its own timetable. For optimal healing, it is best to cooperate.

At this point, my brother's medical prognosis was dismal, with all available treatments exhausted. It was a waiting game that is undeniably the hardest for humanity. Psalm 46:10 says, "Be still, and know that I am God." Unfortunately, being still is antithetical to humanity's programmed thinking to "Do something now!" At any given moment, instructing God on His next plan of action is incredibly easy, and waiting is never a consideration. As I imagined my brother's thought process in the "be still" command, my dilemma to "go on a cruise or stay" seemed trivial compared to the eternal thoughts my brother was entertaining. After much contemplation and prayer, I decided to attend my class reunion. My brother would have found the idea absurd for me stay on his account.

Ordinarily, I love a good time with lots of laughter and jokes. As much as I tried not to grieve, sadness was a constant companion on this cruise. I socialized with classmates, but on a superficial level. Deep down, my greatest desire was to have as minimal interaction as possible. I relied on my first-grade friends to carry conversations and be my security blanket. I was as vulnerable as Linus on *Charlie Brown*. The classmates didn't notice the difference, since I had not seen many of them in thirty years. People are generally content to accept a person's disposition without suspecting a troubled soul lurking within. No one asked, and I did not explain my less-than-enthusiastic demeanor.

In the midst of the celebratory environment, an elated someone declared that we were a "great class." While deeply committed to my somber mood, this comment struck me as odd. As diligently as I searched, I found absolutely no greatness. In my mind, greatness was expressing God and revealing Him so others might relish His excellence as well. We were not praising God for provision or health and strength. We were simply lifting ourselves above other high school classes, people who had not organized a trip and garnered average participation. I was not sensing greatness here.

In the midst of my "just want to be left alone" attitude, the Holy Spirit pricked my heart to act and speak. My mouth opened, and I heard myself questioning others. "Are we great for coming on a cruise?" I found myself interacting with others and describing true greatness.

In my mind, greatness would have been expressing gratitude for the many blessings we had received from attending this high school and for giving back to our impoverished community. Our high school was in a predominantly African-American community in rural Georgia. In fact, our county was ranked the poorest, last among the 159 counties in the state. However, what my community lacked in material wealth excelled in love and support. As a result, many in our class reaped the benefits of a small-town upbringing and experienced success in various endeavors. Nevertheless, the fact remained that our high school was the poorest, while we were celebrating unashamedly on a party cruise line.

Regardless of my current emotional state, the embers burned within me to give God glory in all things and at all times (mourning included). I announced to the exuberant class that now was the time for us to make a difference, to return to our alma mater. Our goal was to demonstrate true greatness by delivering a message of hope, faith, and belief. We launched a scholarship fundraiser to accompany our words with action. We committed to an unprecedented $5,000 in scholarship awards—an unimpressive amount to some, but remarkable for a community that struggled economically.

As soon as I returned from the cruise, so did reality. The days with my brother were numbered, but we were grateful for each day that he was with us. Deep down, we were afraid of him leaving and felt incapable of filling the shoes he would leave behind. We struggled with God's greatness. We praised Him for every positive test result and each new day. We questioned His wisdom and lovingkindness with every setback. We wanted to define God's greatness on our terms, based on present circumstances. But His patience and faithfulness were unwavering as we traveled this uncertain path.

Since I was the one who challenged the class to greatness on the cruise, I had to initiate the fundraising. What had I done? Why couldn't I have just kept quiet? Each time I reached out for assistance, I encountered resistance. I needed all my time and energy for my brother, not a scholarship campaign. The tension between holding on to a passing life and helping others in this life became my new reality. And somewhere in the middle of it all, I wanted to give up.

With Thanksgiving approaching, my brother's suffering became unbearable. We made peace with God and begged for mercy. Enough. We decided to trust God, both with our brother and with our own insecurities and fears. Anthony passed away peacefully on Thanksgiving night, and we trusted that he was in the presence of the Lord. We planned a funeral service that emphasized God's glory and not my brother, just as he preferred.

After taking time to somewhat recover, I shifted my attention to the scholarship, unable to escape my words spoken on the cruise. Others started to take an interest and progress ensued. At the conclusion of the fundraising process, we had raised $5,100. We presented three scholarships and vowed to return the next year with more money. Members of the Class of 1982 were praising God, refusing to accept any accolades for themselves. The community was stunned that a class returned with a generous gift. As a result, other classes were motivated to do likewise.

God works on behalf of His people all the time, even during extremely difficult times. I will always link the goodness that arose from a hesitant class reunion with my brother's passing away. God taught me not to allow my circumstances to circumvent the goodness that He desires for His people. God in His infinite wisdom trained my wandering eye to look for Him and His goodness at all times. Also, God confirmed that He is capable of working miracles through my feebleness. My role is to make myself available as a willing vessel for His use during times of both weakness and strength. Romans 8:28 became a living applicable verse: "And we know that in all things God works for the good of those who love him, who have been called according to his purpose."

To God be the glory for the great things He has done.

Gwen Burno *resides in Fairview, Texas, with her husband and three children. Her education includes a BBA from Georgia State University, MBA from Alaska Pacific University, and MA in Biblical Studies from Dallas Theological Seminary. She serves as the Spiritual Development Leader at Rockbridge Bible Church in Allen, Texas. Her passion is encouraging others to know God through His Word and live victoriously. Her current pursuit includes developing her Christian Life Coach and Speaking business. Contact information is* **GEBurno@gmail.com.**

Thoughts to Ponder
from Should I Go or Should I Stay?

1. Even though visible evidence is absent, God works during waiting periods.

2. God's love is sufficient to cover my fears and insecurities.

3. We shouldn't close our hearts to God's goodness during our saddest or weakest moments.

How do you respond when God says to wait?

I remain confident of this: I will see the goodness of the Lord in the land of the living. Wait for the Lord; be strong and take heart and wait for the Lord. — Psalm 27:13–14

What Is Wrong with You?

by Virginia Grounds

Virginia, what is wrong with you?

A co-worker asked me that question many years ago. My answer was, "I don't know what is wrong with me. I just know I am miserable."

She pointed her finger and laughed. "Oh, I know what is wrong with you. God has you under conviction."

Conviction—what did that mean? I was too embarrassed to tell her I had no idea what she was talking about. But that was where my journey of faith began. I was twenty-nine years old.

There were no computers, much less Google and Wikipedia. So the old-fashioned way of finding a word definition was through a Webster's paper dictionary. This is the meaning I found: "Being convinced; strong belief. To be convicted." Well, gee—that was certainly helpful. However, with that definition, I had to ask, "What am I being convinced of?" I examined what was missing in my life. I questioned what I believed about God. Until then, all I knew of God was rote prayers before meals when I was a child, back when I was hunting Easter eggs at church with my siblings. As I searched, God gently led me to the answer.

Let me back up a few years. The twenties were difficult years for my young daughter and me. As a single mom, I struggled with all the normal things a single mom struggles with—time, money, relationships, and parenting. I also struggled with grief. My mother died when I was twenty-four and my dad when I was twenty-seven. Since I did not have faith in God to keep me grounded, I was a miserable, angry, and hurting person. Relationships were destroyed by my personal pain.

Then I met and married my husband, whose family was made up of faithful believers and prayer warriors. They were different from what I knew, and as time went by, I longed for what they had, even though I couldn't tell you what it was.

Shortly after our marriage, I worked for a company where the leadership offered a weekly Bible study. Being raised and taught to be a "good girl," I thought I should attend the study. Little did I know what God had in store. The leader gave each of us a Bible and taught from the book of Revelation.

Revelation? Really?

When my husband and I were dating, I asked what his family believed.

He told me some things, but what stood out to me was when he said, "They believe Jesus will come again, and believers will be taken up with Him."

My reaction was disbelief. "You have got to be kidding me. That is the most ridiculous statement I have ever heard."

So how did God get my attention to lead me to Jesus? He did it by putting me in a study of the book of Revelation to learn about the time when Jesus will return. I became fascinated and couldn't get enough of knowing God and His Word. One day while at the grocery store, I saw a book by Hal Lindsey titled, *The Late Great Planet Earth*. As I read and read, I couldn't put the book down. One night while home alone, I read the last chapter and there on the last page was the prayer for salvation. A lightbulb went on inside, and I thought, *This is it. This is what I have been looking for.*

I got on my knees by the bed and prayed to receive Jesus.

From that moment, God gave me a hunger to know Him more and a thirst for wisdom from the Bible that is still with me today. In that moment by my bed, my life was dramatically changed. God has proven Himself to me repeatedly, beginning with the teaching that you don't mock God or His people. He used the very thing I had mocked to draw me to Him. He ignited fire in my heart and hunger and thirst for His Word that has never been extinguished. It is still my greatest joy to study the Bible, to teach, and to know Jesus and the Word of God.

That is where my trust-building journey of faith began.

Fast forward to today. Look up the word *conviction* on the Internet using the Merriam-Webster Dictionary website, and you will find a more descriptive definition than I found all those years ago. It says conviction is: "1. The act or process of finding a person guilty of a crime especially in a court of law. 2. The act of convincing a person of error or of compelling the admission of a truth. 3. The state of being convinced of error or compelled to admit the truth. 4. A strong persuasion or belief. The state of being convinced."

This would have been helpful to know years ago, but it still raises questions of what this means in relation to God and faith. People need to attend a Bible-teaching church and read the Bible for themselves to find the answer for what it means to be "under conviction" from a biblical perspective. Let me break it down for you.

- *The act or process of finding a person guilty of a crime especially in a court of law.* Just as justice must be served in a court of law, justice must be served dividing evil from good from a spiritual perspective. God is the Righteous Judge who sent Jesus to reveal that none are righteous without Him. All have sinned and have fallen short of the glory of God (Romans 3:23).

- *The act of convincing a person of error or of compelling the admission of a truth.* Sin must be identified and acknowledged in our lives. We must understand that we cannot be pure without the cleansing blood of Christ, who sacrificed His life for you and me.

- *A strong persuasion or belief. The state of being convinced.* Once we admit our sinful state, ask forgiveness, and invite Jesus into our lives as our Savior, we begin our trust-building journey of faith, believing in Him, having been convinced of the eternal life-saving grace of God, the gift freely given.

In the book of John, we discover that Jesus not only saves us from our sin but also convicts us by His Spirit in a way that we are confronted and weighed down. "When he comes, he will prove the world to be in the wrong about sin and righteousness and judgment" (John 16:8). Convicting the world about sin refers to people's unbelief and their failure to put their trust in Jesus. Only through research and Bible reading was I able to discover this truth about conviction. Only through the boldness of a believing friend was I made aware of my condition and my need.

Therefore, knowing the following verse was crucial for understanding how much God loved and pursued me: "For God so loved the world that he gave his one and only Son, that whoever believes in him shall not perish but have eternal life. For God did not send his Son into the world to condemn the world, but to save the world through him" (John 3:16–17).

Knowing Jesus is a choice that people can only make for

themselves. Billy Graham said it best: "Our families cannot choose Christ for us. Our friends cannot do it. God is a great God, but even God can't make the decision for us—we have to make our own choice."[1]

I made that choice, but I was a young adult in my late twenties before I determined to know Jesus. I had been under conviction for eight years and didn't know it. At the age of twenty-one, I visited church with a co-worker. From that moment on, I had an unsettled feeling in my soul. God called to me there, but I didn't recognize His voice. So because of poor advice from someone close to me, I walked away and never returned to that church. The price paid, not only for me but also for my daughter, was years of misery without my understanding why. Yet God never gave up on me. He just kept wooing me to come to Him until finally someone got right in my face, pointed a finger, and told me what I needed to hear. "God has you under conviction." So I searched for answers. I searched for Jesus. I wanted Him as my Savior but didn't know how to go about it. Then I read a book that explained much of what I had longed to know. At the end of the book, the author wrote what to pray to accept Jesus and be saved. It changed my life, and it can do the same for you.

God has taught me so much through the years of my faith journey, and the lessons learned, from the beginning of the journey to Him, still apply today.

- *You don't mock God.* He used the very thing I had mocked to draw me to Him through studying His Book from the very last chapter. Yes, Jesus will come again.
- *You don't walk away from God when He calls you to Himself.* He knows right where you are, and He knows your heart. I had the opportunity to come to Jesus at the age of twenty-one, but I walked away for eight miserable years. So much regret, but so great a grace and forgiveness.
- *God doesn't give up on you.* Even though He allowed me to walk away by my choice, my will, God didn't stop trying to get my attention. He never wavered in His purpose, not only to save me but also to use me for His service. And I am still

serving Him today. It is still my heart's desire. Praise God for His unwavering, pursuing love.

What is your heart's desire? Do you feel like something is wrong with you? Don't be like me and turn away from the *first* opportunity to accept Jesus as Savior or to return to Him. Don't be like me and suffer for years without knowing why. Turn to Jesus now. Your life will never be the same. What He did for me, He will do for you.

Virginia Grounds *is a wife, mom, and grandmother. She is also a speaker, author, Bible teacher, and former radio host. She served for twenty-five years on the women's ministry teaching team at her church in Plano, Texas, and served with her husband in full-time ministry for seventeen years. Her books,* Facing Fears, Quenching Flames, *and* Rock Solid Trust *are both available on Amazon or her website. Read Virginia's blogs and hear her radio broadcasts at*

MajesticInspirations.com,
Contact: **VGrounds@MajesticInspirations.com**

Thoughts to Ponder
from What Is Wrong with You?

1. God is a pursuer of souls.

2. We are often convicted by God so we
    will seek answers.

3. With God there is always hope.

What is your heart's desire?
Do you long to know more of Jesus?

[Nothing] will be able to separate us from the love of God
that is in Christ Jesus our Lord. — Romans 8:39

Beliefs from God's Word

We believe . . . that the Bible is the verbally inspired Word of God and without mistakes as originally written. It is the complete revelation of His will for salvation and the only unfailing rule of faith and practice for the Christian life.

We believe . . . in one God, Creator of all things, eternally existing in three persons: Father, Son, and Holy Spirit, and that these three are co-eternal and of equal dignity and power.

We believe . . . in the deity of Jesus Christ; His miraculous conception by the Holy Spirit; His virgin birth; His sinless life; His substitutionary death on a cross; His bodily resurrection; His ascension to the right hand of the Father; and His personal, imminent return.

We believe . . . that man was created by and for God; that by man's disobeying God, every person incurred spiritual death, which is separation from God, and physical death as a consequence; and that all people are sinners by nature and practice.

We believe . . . the Lord Jesus Christ died for our sins, and all who believe in Him are declared righteous because of His sacrificial death and are, therefore, in right relationship with God.

We believe . . . in the present ministry of the Holy Spirit indwelling all believers and thus enabling and empowering the life and ministry of the believer.

We believe . . . in the bodily resurrection of everyone who has lived, the everlasting blessedness of those in right relationship with God, and the everlasting punishment of those who have rejected God's forgiveness in His Son.

God's Good News for You

Now that you have read these stories of great faith, you may want to know how you can have this same kind of faith. We have Good News for you.

He loves you!
For God so loved the world that he gave his one and only Son, that whoever believes in him shall not perish but have eternal life. — John 3:16

He wants to meet your need.
Your iniquities have separated you from your God; your sins have hidden his face from you, so that he will not hear. — Isaiah 59:2

God made him who had no sin to be sin for us, so that in him we might become the righteousness of God. — 2 Corinthians 5:21

He offers you a free gift!
The wages of sin is death, but the gift of God is eternal life in Christ Jesus our Lord. — Romans 6:23

How to receive this gift:
If you declare with your mouth, "Jesus is Lord," and believe in your heart that God raised him from the dead, you will be saved. — Romans 10:9

Jesus, I recognize I have sinned and need You. I believe You are the Son of God, that You died on the cross for my sin, rose from the dead and now sit at the right hand of God. I trust You alone and choose to follow You. Thank you for forgiving me of my sin and giving me eternal life. In Jesus' name, amen.

If you have chosen to receive God's gift or would like more information, please contact us at **info@RoaringLambs.org**. We would love to hear from you!

Share with Us

Roaring Lambs is working on our next volume of *Stories of Roaring Faith*, a book of testimonies designed to lead a nonbeliever to faith in Jesus Christ and to encourage the followers of Jesus. We would love to receive your testimony. Please submit via email your typed, double-spaced, approximately 3,000-word story.

Email: **info@RoaringLambs.org**

Please submit your testimony as soon as possible. You will receive a Release Form giving us permission to edit and consider your testimony for a future volume.

In addition, you may be invited as a guest on our radio show, *A Time to Dream*, which also features life-changing testimonies.

Let God use your story by writing, submitting, and sharing what He has done for you.

Roaring Lambs Ministries is a 501(c)(3), which exists on tax deductible donations. We would welcome any gifts to sustain our ministry to equip believers to better communicate their faith. Donations may be made online at **RoaringLambs.org** or mailed to Roaring Lambs, 17110 Dallas Parkway, Suite 260, Dallas, TX 75248.

There are many ways to give to Roaring Lambs: check, credit card, gifts of stock or real estate, or planned gifts by will or trust. Roaring Lambs can help with any of the above by working with your attorney or accountant.

Give, and it will be given to you. A good measure, pressed down, shaken together and running over, will be poured into your lap. For with the measure you use, it will be measured to you. — Luke 6:38

About the Editors

Donna Skell

With a heart for God, people, and business, Donna stays active in the Christian community. She has been involved with this ministry since its inception and came on staff in 2008. Donna oversees all Roaring Lambs events and Bible studies. She co-hosts an international radio show called *A Time to Dream*, airing four times a week on three platforms. The program features powerful faith stories. By collecting these amazing stories, Roaring Lambs Ministries has produced three volumes of *Stories of Roaring Faith*. She especially enjoys speaking to ladies' groups, churches, and retreats. Her rich Jewish heritage and her study of God's Word enhance her insight into the issues involved in Christian faith and living.

In addition to her work with Roaring Lambs, Donna serves on the Christian Women in Media Advisory Committee, and the Collin County Christian Prayer Breakfast Committee.

DSkell@RoaringLambs.org

Belinda McBride

Answering God's call at the age of nine to become a "missionary," Belinda's mission was to touch others with the Good News of Jesus Christ. Her passion has been equipping believers to effectively live life with hope, purpose, and strength. She has done this as a pastor's daughter, pastor's wife, administrator, Bible study teacher, speaker, and writer.

She has served in many churches and ministries, including Hope for the Heart, Marketplace Ministries, and Roaring Lambs. Belinda's great joy is her husband, four daughters and fifteen grandchildren. She currently resides in Carrollton, Texas and is Director of Operations with Roaring Lambs Ministries. She can be contacted at

BMcBride@RoaringLambs.org.

Lisa Burkhardt Worley

Lisa Burkhardt Worley is an award-winning author and speaker, and is the Director of Special Projects for Roaring Lambs Ministries. She is also founder of "Pearls of Promise Ministries." Lisa has authored, co-authored, or co-edited eight books, *The Only Father I Ever Knew*, the *Pearls of Promise* devotional, *If I Only Had*, *The Most Powerful P: A Child's Introduction to the Power of Prayer*, *The Most Powerful P Activity Book and Prayer Journal*, and three volumes of *Stories of Roaring Faith*.

Lisa is a former television sportscaster, and now co-hosts an international weekly radio show with Donna Skell called, *A Time to Dream*, airing four times a week on three platforms. Lisa earned a Master of Theological Studies degree from Perkins School of Theology.

LBWorley@RoaringLambs.org
PearlsofPromiseMinistries.com

Dr. Sherry Ryan

Dr. Sherry D. Ryan is a retired Associate Professor of Information Technology and Decision Sciences at the University of North Texas. She received her Ph.D in Information Systems from the University of Texas at Arlington and an MBA from the University of Southern California. Prior to earning her doctorate, she worked for IBM, teaching courses and speaking at national conferences.

She has published numerous academic journal articles, conference proceedings, and is currently working on a book. Sherry has two children, one granddaughter, and one grandson. She manages the Roaring Lambs website, is passionate about missions, and is on the Board of Directors for "His Appointed Time Ministries."

Ministry@RoaringLambs.org

Frank Ball

For ten years, Frank Ball directed North Texas Christian Writers to help members improve their writing and storytelling skills. In 2011, he founded Story Help Groups and joined the Roaring Writers ministry seven years later to encourage and equip all Christians to tell their life-changing stories. He has taught at writer's conferences and churches across the U.S. and Canada. Besides writing his own books, he does ghostwriting, copy editing, and graphic design to help others publish high-quality books.

As Pastor of Biblical Research and Writing for three years, he wrote sermons, teaching materials, and hundreds of devotions. He coaches writers, writes blogs, and is a panelist on The Writer's View. His first book, *Eyewitness: The Life of Christ Told in One Story*, is a compilation of biblical information on the life of Christ in a chronological story that reads like a novel. His website is
www.FrankBall.org.

Made in the USA
San Bernardino, CA
07 September 2018